BEYOND
DISRUPTION

BEYOND

DISRUPTION

Innovate and Achieve Growth *without* Displacing Industries, Companies, or Jobs

W. Chan Kim
Renée Mauborgne

Harvard Business Review Press

Boston, Massachusetts

Library of Congress Cataloging-in-Publication Data

Names: Kim, W. Chan, author. | Mauborgne, Renée, author.
Title: Beyond disruption : innovate and achieve growth without displacing
    industries, companies, or jobs / W. Chan Kim, Renée Mauborgne.
Description: Boston, Massachusetts : Harvard Business Review Press, [2023] |
    Includes index.
Identifiers: LCCN 2022037071 (print) | LCCN 2022037072 (ebook) |
    ISBN 9781647821326 (hardcover) | ISBN 9781647821333 (epub)
Subjects: LCSH: Technological innovations. | Success in business. |
    Economic development. | Business ethics. | Disruptive technologies.
Classification: LCC HD45 .K538 2023 (print) | LCC HD45 (ebook) | DDC
    658.4/063—dc23/eng/20230110
LC record available at https://lccn.loc.gov/2022037071
LC ebook record available at https://lccn.loc.gov/2022037072

ISBN: 978-1-64782-132-6
eISBN: 978-1-64782-133-3

*Grounded optimists have the advantage because
they believe a solution is possible and
a better world can be built*

Contents

Preface

All the disruption in this world has left many of us and our organizations broken and tired, not to mention anxious.

In business and the economy, we yearn for another way, one with less destruction and more hope. A path beyond disruption, where economic and social good are not trade-offs, but where business and society can move in lockstep and thrive together.

In this book, we lay out such a path in innovation and growth. It's a path to new industries, new jobs, and profitable growth but without the shuttered companies, hurt communities, or lost jobs of disruption in its wake.

It's what we call *non*disruptive creation that allows us to innovate and grow without disruption and social pain.

What is nondisruptive creation, and why does it matter? How does it complement disruption and why is it likely to grow in importance in the future? What are its distinctive advantages to companies and our society? And how can you achieve it?

If you want to be an innovator who aims to achieve both profitable growth and social good and are not satisfied with achieving just one or the other, we invite you to join us on our journey as we set out to answer these questions in this book.

The idea of nondisruptive creation is borne out of a long research journey. It began over thirty years ago, at the University of Michigan Business School in Ann Arbor, when we started what has essentially become a three-decades-long conversation on strategy and innovation. Our conversation took place sometimes on campus, sometimes on our usual walks in the Arboretum. And it continued at INSEAD, both on campus at the Blue Ocean Strategy Institute and on our long walks through the forest of Fontainebleau, France.

The gist of our conversations went something like this:

"How can we define strategy in simple terms?"

"Many believe that strategy is about competing; the goal is to beat the competition."

"Indeed, the strategic focus of many corporate executives is on outperforming rivals in their existing industries. That's driven by zero-sum thinking where one wins at the expense of the other."

"That's the logical framing when industry players fight for a share of the existing pie."

"But if *creating* a new pie is the focus, and we know how to do so, the view of strategy can be broadened to embrace non-zero-sum thinking, which the prevailing theory and practice of strategy whose focus is on *competing* largely lacks."

"Similarly, the view of innovation is also shaped by win-lose thinking. A key innovation theory like creative destruction, for example, states that to grow, you need to create, but to create the new, you need to destroy the existing."

"And disruption, especially as it has come to be commonly understood by leaders and innovators, is basically about displacing existing companies, jobs, and industries."

"How can we go beyond such win-lose thinking, which largely drives the current theory and practice of innovation?"

Having published our thoughts and findings on non-zero-sum thinking in strategy—culminating in our book *Blue Ocean Strategy* and later *Blue Ocean Shift*, we received numerous inquiries and comments from various academics and the practice community to extend our research further into the field of innovation. Their feedback inspired us to push the frontier of our research in innovation beyond non-zero-sum thinking to embrace positive-sum thinking where no one is made worse off. We reasoned that such research would have important implications for business and society; if we can achieve profitable growth without incurring disruptive social costs, business and society could progress more harmoniously. And so we dove into this, coming to an understanding of what we call nondisruptive creation and how managers can harness the power of this new way of thinking about innovation—and this book reports our findings.

This is how our research journey, first to the blue ocean and now to nondisruptive creation, has evolved. With positive-sum thinking, like innovating the new without destroying or disrupting the existing, we believe we can complement existing theories on innovation and help build a world of business that is more agreeable with society.

———————

Reflecting a long research journey, with many struggles but with fond memories and everlasting gratitude.

Chan and Renée

Part One

Nondisruptive Creation

What It Is and Why It Matters

Chapter One

Innovation and Growth *without* Disruption

The concert was held on a star-filled night in Las Vegas on September 21, 2018, as part of the event Life Is Beautiful. And that night was just that—beautiful. The rock group Greta Van Fleet headlined the performance, which was hosted by the music industry veteran Jason Flom's new venture, the Church of Rock & Roll.

This concert, however, was different. It was unlike any rock concert ever before played. When the music started, it was as if time had stopped. As the opening notes blasted forth, not a single person in the room felt anything other than awe. The audience was left speechless. Hair stood up on the backs of people's necks. Tears ran down people's cheeks.

Many in attendance had never been to a rock concert until that night—never swayed with the audience and felt the euphoria many of us feel when a band starts to play. What brought them to the concert that night? What made this concert distinctive? Was it the band, the songs played, or even the venue? It was none of these. It was the audience.

What made that concert audience unique is that half its members were functionally deaf. But at this concert the deaf experienced music just as the nondeaf did. While the music played, not only those who could hear but those who couldn't, or who had struggled to hear music until that night, started swaying with the music. And as this fact sank in, smiles spread like wildfire across the faces in attendance. The first deaf rock concert ever played in America and arguably in the world was played that night.

What made it possible? Music: Not Impossible (M:NI). Mick Ebeling, Daniel Belquer, and their team, the creators of M:NI, developed the first-of-a-kind wearable vibrotactile device for the deaf. It's a cool black vest, to be worn over a shirt, that contains a full sound system of twenty-four sleek, lightweight vibrators strategically placed inside at the waist, the neck, and the shoulders, produced with the support of Avnet. Think of a wet-suit vest and an added ankle band like the one on a surfboard that keeps the surfer from losing the board in a fall. The vibrators have different levels of intensity and different frequencies to match the nuances of the music played and the varying intensities of the instruments.

Here is a surprising thing: Did you know that people don't actually hear with their ears? Sound—which is really vibration—enters the brain through the ears, but it is in fact the brain that creates the effect of hearing. So if you fall and hit your head in a particular way, you can lose your hearing even if your ears weren't hurt. Ebeling and his team reasoned that although the ears of the deaf don't perceive vibrational sound, they might be able to find a different way to let vibrations in so that the brain could pick them up. Which

4

is exactly what they did. They used the skin instead of the ear as the medium for vibrations to reach the brain.

While it was commonly accepted that experiencing music was impossible for the functionally deaf, M:NI showed that it was not only *not* impossible, but also *possible*—and done. In America alone, more than a million people are estimated to be functionally deaf. These are people for whom the world has largely gone silent. Think of how much pleasure and joy music brings to the world. Play a song, and even a toddler is likely to bop and sway and smile without prodding. With M:NI, the deaf, too, can now have the pleasure of experiencing live music. M:NI is now scaling the delivery of their vibrotactile offering across the globe from a music festival in London to opera in Philadelphia to the Brazilian Symphony Orchestra and silent discos at Lincoln Center to reach out to everyone, the deaf and hearing alike. Their tagline, "good vibes for all."

We thought about M:NI's innovation. It's clearly not incremental. Nor is it disruptive—a catchword that has come to dominate the innovation space. To the contrary, M:NI created an opportunity for people who probably never imagined they would be able to experience music. It did not invade, destroy, or displace any existing market or industry. It created *without disruption.*

Is M:NI an anomaly when it comes to innovation? No. Think of something far more common in the world today that is hardly given a second thought: corrective eyeglasses. Before glasses came along, people with challenged vision—whether nearsighted or farsighted— had to live with compromised sight. According to the "World Report on Vision" published by the World Health Organization, at least 2.2 billion people around the world are visually impaired.[1] Think of the nearsighted child who can't read a blackboard from the back of a classroom, or the farsighted adult who struggles to read a book. Both impairments greatly hamper people's learning and ability to economically participate and function as productive individuals. Then they put on a pair of glasses, and the world is revealed in a new light. Blades of grass! Oh, my gosh, I never knew you could see them! Is that what is written on the blackboard? No wonder I never understood the lesson. Learning is now so much easier.

Eyeglasses created an opportunity that never existed before. Like M:NI, they were not an incremental innovation. They created a new industry. But again like M:NI, they were also not disruptive. They didn't destroy any established industry or displace any established players. They only created growth, clear vision for people, and lots of new jobs in all the companies that produced them. Today the industry is worth more than $100 billion. When you think about it, there are many other examples, including microfinance for the billions of poor people, that were created without disrupting or displacing anyone.

This got us thinking. For the past twenty years, "disruption" has been the battle cry of business: Disrupt this. Disrupt that. Disrupt or die.[2] Calls for disruption have rung out across Silicon Valley, major corporate boardrooms, the media, and business conferences around the globe.[3] Corporate leaders have continually been warned that the only way to survive, succeed, and grow is to disrupt their industries or even their own companies. Not surprisingly, many have come to see *disruption* as a near-synonym for *innovation*.

But is disruption the only way to innovate and grow? And is it necessarily the best way? As our research and these cases suggest, the answer is no. It may be what people talk about, it's certainly important, and it's all around us. But the overriding focus on disruption has led us to largely overlook another avenue of innovation and growth—one that we would argue is at least as important. That avenue involves the creation of new markets without disruption or displacement—what we've come to think of as *nondisruptive* cre-

6

ation.[4] Nondisruptive creation creates new industries without leaving failed companies, lost jobs, and destroyed markets in its wake.[5] It offers the immense potential to innovate new markets where none existed before. If we could better understand this other form of market-creating innovation and how it works, we would be better equipped to achieve it.

And so our research questions began: Is nondisruptive creation about scientific or technological innovation or new-to-the-world products? Or is it something different? If different, is it applicable to all regions of the globe or only to certain geographic areas, such as bottom-of-the-pyramid markets where a lack of economic development may mean there are few industries to be disrupted? Relatedly, is it applicable to all levels of the socioeconomic pyramid of a region or only to any specific level? Our answer to these questions was that nondisruptive creation *can't* be defined as inventive or new technology or new-to-the-world innovation or confined to any specific geographic market or socioeconomic level. It is a distinct new concept.

Three Ideas That Changed the World

You may not have given much thought to sanitary napkins (and that holds true regardless of your gender), but that one innovation both created a brand-new industry and has had a substantial impact on the opportunity scope for half the world's population. Today most women in developed countries take sanitary napkins for granted. Every month women of menstruating age, from as young as nine to as old as the late fifties, reach for them to deal with the inconvenience (and messiness) of their monthly cycles. But that wasn't always the case.

7

Prior to the modern sanitary napkin, no industry or market addressed this problem. Instead, many women resorted to nonmarket solutions such as used cloth or old rags they had on hand, or even sheep's wool. These were often unsanitary and could cause infection or other health issues. And the cloth, lacking high absorbency, an impenetrable backing, and a systematic way of being secured to undergarments, was also often uncomfortable, shifted when worn, and led to "accidents" of visible spotting and leakage. To avoid the embarrassment of this problem, girl students often stayed away from school during their monthly cycles, thereby losing a few days of school every month.

All that changed when the nondisruptive market for sanitary napkins was created.[6] With sanitary napkins, girls could go to school and play sports without worry, and women could more easily work and provide for their families. The sanitary napkin took much of the stigma and dread out of women's menstrual cycles. We might even argue that it went a long way toward freeing women to foster their careers, education, and even health prospects. Social good and economic good went hand in hand with that new industry. Today the sanitary-napkin industry generates revenues of more than $22 billion a year.

Relatively recently, Arunachalam Muruganantham created a brand-new market for sanitary pads for women in rural India, where the situation is very different: speaking about menstruation— even between husbands and wives—continues to be largely socially taboo. Muruganantham's creation was a very simple, small padmaking machine that's sold directly to women in the villages, who then sell the sanitary pads they produce directly to other local women. So far, his machines have created about 5,300 for-profit microbusinesses for rural women, overcoming an impossible distribution channel and, more important, a taboo subject that affected half the Indian population but that nobody used to talk about. That kind of opportunity still exists in many areas of the world. What we take for granted may not be the norm in the rest of the world. And again, the market Muruganantham has created is nondisruptive and huge. There was no existing market offering in the rural villages of India, where more than 200 million women—more than the total US female population—live.

Now think of microfinance. Some forty years ago, that industry didn't exist, but today it is a multibillion-dollar industry. Microfinance has helped change the lives of many of the world's extremely poor, who today still number nearly 700 million people. How? By ushering in the end of a long era of financial apartheid for people living on less than a few dollars a day or even less than a dollar a day.

The industry was founded by Muhammad Yunus, who at the time was the head of the economics department at the University of Chittagong, in Bangladesh. In his university courses, he theorized about sums in the millions of dollars. But after a particularly acute famine swept through Bangladesh, leaving countless poor people dying in the streets right before him, Yunus set out to understand what was at the root of extreme poverty.

What he found was that extreme poverty had nothing to do with the things he taught in economics class, or with people being lazy or stupid. In their small one-room, dirt-floored huts, with no tables, chairs, windows, or running water, Yunus found industrious people who squatted on the floor, carefully doing complex tasks such as making bamboo stools or weaving baskets or sleeping mats for hours on end, earning barely enough to stay alive.

With income so low, the extremely poor would never be able to save a penny or invest in expanding their economic base. Any hope for a better life often rested on pennies. But no bank or financial institution existed to cater to the credit needs of these people.

Conventional banks had simply ignored the poor, whom they deemed unsuitable as borrowers.

Microfinance changed that. In 1983, Yunus officially established Grameen Bank, the first microcredit bank in the world, which lent tiny sums to the poor. By solving a long overlooked and unaddressed problem, microcredit enabled people who had previously been denied access to capital to create new microbusinesses, new jobs, higher standards of living, and hope.

This nondisruptive move created the new market of microfinance without replacing any other industry. Microfinance has since ballooned into a multibillion-dollar industry with a staggering 98 percent loan-repayment rate and plenty of room for future growth. As Yunus has noted, microcredit may not eliminate poverty altogether, but it has ended it for many and reduces its severity for others, building a fairer and more prosperous future for all.

That brings us to Elmo, Big Bird, and adorable Cookie Monster. The world learned about these fabulous Muppets through Sesame Street, which created a brand-new opportunity for the world's future—namely, children.

Sesame Street started in America and rolled out first to Western Europe and other developed countries and then to developing countries. Today the program helps children in more than 150 countries, from America to Afghanistan, Japan, and Brazil. It has even reached the middle of the Serengeti and, recently, children in refugee camps.

As most of us who have children know, Sesame Street teaches preschool children how to count, name their colors and shapes, and recognize the letters of the alphabet. More than that, it shows preschoolers how to be kind to one another, to accept differences, to control impulses and concentrate. But the best part is that children have so much fun watching the program, with the lovable

Muppets and songs, that they don't even realize how much they're learning. But parents do, which is why they love it too. It's the antithesis of what many people associate with education. It seduces and amuses as it educates the very young.

Sesame Street did not displace preschools, libraries, or even parents reading bedtime stories to their children. Rather, it created a brand-new opportunity for children and learning by unlocking the nondisruptive market of preschool edutainment that for the most part had not existed before. Today, preschool edutainment is a multibillion-dollar industry. And Sesame Street has become the most successful, longest-running children's television show in history, winning 189 Emmy Awards and 11 Grammys.

What Can We Learn?

This concept we have come to think of as *nondisruptive creation* has three distinctive characteristics. First, it can be generated by a scientific invention or a technology-driven innovation—as in the case of sanitary pads for women. But it can also be generated *without* science or technology-driven innovation, as was the case with microfinance, or with a new combination or application of existing technology, as was the case with Sesame Street, which leveraged the existing technology of television to unlock the preschool edutainment industry.[7] This is good news for many entrepreneurs, executives, and companies that lack the wherewithal or the appetite to invest in scientific or technological innovations. As Daniel Belquer of M:NI has noted, "Each individual part already existed before, but these [technological] elements—hardware, software, and wearables—were combined in a new way to produce M:NI."

Second, nondisruptive creation is not limited to any specific region or socioeconomic standing. It's applicable to any geographic area of the world, be that developed markets or bottom-of-the-pyramid markets. Sesame Street, sanitary pads, and M:NI were all created in, and initially for, developed economies.[8] But microfinance and the sanitary-pad machines of India were created in and initially for bottom-of-the-pyramid markets.[9] Opportunities for nondisruptive creation exist in all areas of the world. They also exist at all levels of the socioeconomic pyramid in a region. While corrective eyeglasses or sanitary napkins were initially for the upper tier of socioeconomic standing, microfinance or the sanitary-pad machine of India was initially for the lower tier. The concept is open to us all.

Third, nondisruptive creation is not the same as new-to-the-world innovation, which can just as easily be disruptive as nondisruptive. Consider Muruganantham's machine that created a brand-new market, jobs, and strong growth without displacing any established player or market. His offering was new and nondisruptive to that area. But the same machine, if sold in developed areas where sanitary pads are easily accessible by market players, could be disruptive to them. Hence Muruganantham's nondisruptive creation is a new-to-the-*area* innovation. By contrast, Sesame Street is an example of new-to-the-*world* innovation, because the preschool edutainment industry it pioneered was nondisruptive across the globe.[10]

What all this means is that nondisruptive creation is not the same as, nor should it be confused with, a scientific invention or technological innovation per se, new-to-the-world products or services, or certain geographic markets or socioeconomic demographics, as you'll see throughout this book. It is a distinct concept that can universally be defined as *the creation of a brand-new market outside or beyond the boundaries of existing industries.* It is precisely because the new industry is created *outside* the bounds of existing industries that there is no existing market or established players to be disrupted and fail. Table 1-1 lays out the definition and the three distinctive conceptual characteristics of nondisruptive creation.

TABLE 1-1

Nondisruptive creation as a distinctive innovation concept for growth

Definition	Nondisruptive creation *is* the creation of a brand-new market *outside* or *beyond* existing industry boundaries.
Three distinctive conceptual characteristics	While it can occur with new inventive technology, it also occurs with a new combination or application of existing technology. It *is not* about a scientific invention or technology innovation per se.
	It *can be but doesn't have to be* a new-to-the-world innovation. As an offering that already exists in one area can be brand new when it is offered in other areas, it *often is* a new-to-the-area innovation that creates a brand-new market in an area.
	It *is* applicable to any geographical market of the world, whether a developed or bottom-of-the-pyramid market. Its application *is not limited* to any specific area or level of socioeconomic standing.

Table 1-2 complements table 1-1 with a simple schematic showing the breadth of possible opportunities for nondisruptive creation. As depicted, the applicability of nondisruptive creation is not limited to any specific socioeconomic standing; it can occur at any level from the top to the base of the socioeconomic pyramid in a region. It is this wide applicability that makes nondisruptive creation so relevant to all of us.

TABLE 1-2

Range of nondisruptive creation possibilities

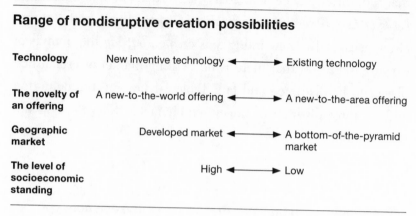

Technology	New inventive technology ◄───► Existing technology	
The novelty of an offering	A new-to-the-world offering ◄───► A new-to-the-area offering	
Geographic market	Developed market ◄───► A bottom-of-the-pyramid market	
The level of socioeconomic standing	High ◄───► Low	

Nondisruptive Creation Has Been All Around Us but Hidden

Although the term *nondisruptive creation* is new, its existence is not. It's a fact of business life—past, present, and future. It applies to for-profits, nonprofits, the public sector, and even government. Nondisruptive opportunities may be as large as the cybersecurity industry or of a far more modest scale, as with M:NI, but the concept is front and center for business.

While Sesame Street is a nonprofit, microfinance is a for-profit (and profitable), as are corrective eyeglasses and sanitary pads. The men's cosmeceutical industry, environmental consulting, e-sports, air-to-ground communication, 3M Post-it Notes, life coaching, and smartphone accessories—not to mention the US government's creation of Space Force—are all examples of nondisruptive creation that unlocked or are unlocking multimillion- and multibillion-dollar new industries and growth, with countless new jobs.

Consider 23andMe, which created the new market of direct-to-consumer genetic testing. Via a saliva sample that customers mail to the company's laboratory in a special kit, individuals can now find their long-lost or previously unknown blood relatives, understand their ancestry, and learn about genetic predispositions such as late-onset Alzheimer's disease, Parkinson's disease, glaucoma, and celiac disease. Previously, most people had no feasible way to know their genetic predispositions. But with the creation of 23andMe, this became possible. Today the company is valued at more than $1 billion.

Or think of the windshield wiper, which enables people to see while driving in rain or snow, which we all take for granted today. Before that? Well, simply turn off your windshield wipers the next rainy day and you'll quickly discover that you can neither see nor drive safely. The windshield wiper created a new market without any disruption, and it made our lives safer in the process.

Even a nondisruptive creation like Halloween pet costumes is now a $500 million industry. It creates lots of smiles with the brand-new opportunity for people to dress up their four-footed family members as irresistibly cute tacos, nurses, and even superheroes.

As these examples show, when you put on the lens of nondisruptive creation, you quickly discover that it has been all around us. A review of the North American Industry Classification System reflects this well. Since 1997, the system has been revised several times to keep pace with industry creation, re-creation, and growth. In these new versions, although disruption is certainly at play, entirely new classifications were also created to recognize the emergence of brand-new, nondisruptive market spaces and industries.[11] Whether in advanced nations or in developing countries, history has shown that nondisruptive creation is a feature of business life.

Yet when it comes to innovation, nondisruptive creation has been overshadowed by a near-obsession with disruption. Disruption as it has come to be widely used and understood in practice—and as we use it here—occurs when an innovation creates a new market that displaces an existing market and the established players in it. *Displacement* is the operative word here, because without displacement, no disruption will occur. So by disruption, we refer to the displacement of an existing market by the innovation of a new one.

As recent research has shown, displacement can occur from both the high and low ends of an existing market.[12] The iPhone, the electronic calculator, the digital camera, and transatlantic air travel, for example, all displaced existing markets from the high end with higher price points. The disrupted industries were the feature phone, the slide rule, the film camera, and the ocean liner, respectively. In contrast, Amazon (versus book retailers), Skype (versus the telecommunications industry), and Craig's List (versus newspaper classifieds) all disrupted existing markets from the low end, with lower-priced or zero-priced offerings—in line with Clayton Christensen's notion of disruptive innovation.

While the term *disruption* was popularized to no small extent by Christensen's influential work on disruptive innovation, we are not referring to low-end or bottom-up disruption, as defined by Christensen.[13] Rather, we use the term in the broader sense: to describe the phenomenon of disruption in which the new displaces the old from both the high and low ends.

Joseph Schumpeter captured the essence of the disruption or displacement phenomenon long ago in his classic description of "creative destruction." Schumpeter, who is widely recognized as the father of innovation, introduced the notion of creative destruction in his book *Capitalism, Socialism, and Democracy*, first published in 1942.[14] Creative destruction, he argued, occurs when an innovation that creates a new market destroys and displaces an existing one.

Until Schumpeter came on the scene, most economists espoused the view that competition and incremental improvements in existing markets are the main spur to economic growth, with the overriding objective of fostering perfect competition. But, in a study of historical business cycles, Schumpeter made an important observation: that although competition and improvements in existing products and services are good, diminishing returns eventually set in as buyers' needs are satisfied and profits are competed away.

For Schumpeter, therefore, the real engine of economic growth is market-creating innovation that generates new kinds of technologies, goods, and services. New technologies may be either inventive ones or new combinations or applications of existing ones. This creation, however, comes with a hitch: as Schumpeter saw it, it was dependent on destruction. In other words, in Schumpeter's worldview, creation and destruction were inextricably linked. Creative destruction, he argued, incessantly destroys the old and creates the new.

The kerosene lamp, for example, creatively destroyed the candle as the predominant source of artificial light; it was later displaced in turn by the new market of incandescent light bulbs, much as the horse-drawn carriage industry gave way to and was displaced by the auto industry. Each new market displaced the old one, creatively increasing the value delivered to buyers, drawing in new buyers, and opening a new growth horizon in the economy.

Schumpeter's creative destruction clearly offers good conceptual ground for explaining the disruption reality that has been unfolding in the business world of today as displacement has been occurring from both top-down and bottom-up directions in existing industries.[15] That said, the word *destruction* is too restrictive for a world in which many existing industry players are indeed disrupted but not necessarily killed or fully displaced.

Think of Uber versus taxis or Amazon versus book retailers. Both companies disrupted existing industries and shifted lots of demand from the old to the new, but they have not destroyed and fully displaced the old, which still exists, though in a much-reduced form.

Thus, we use the term *disruptive creation* to describe the creation of the new that disrupts but doesn't *necessarily* fully displace the old.

In today's disruption reality, Schumpeterian destruction of an existing industry—as in the internal-combustion engine's full displacement of the steam engine—is often the extreme case. To use the term *disruptive creation* is to follow the Schumpeterian notion of new market creation for growth, yet to better reflect and capture the reality, in which the new often coexists with the old, and displacement happens from both the high and low ends of existing markets.[16]

Two Opposite Ends of the Market-Creating Innovation Spectrum

Disruptive creation and nondisruptive creation may be thought of as opposite ends of the innovation spectrum of new-market creation and growth. On one end is nondisruptive creation, which is about creating a new market *outside* or *beyond* existing industry boundaries, while on the other end is disruptive creation, which is about creating a new market *within* the boundaries and expanding them.[17]

A key factor that makes distinguishing between the two important is their differing impacts on the economy and society. With disruptive creation, the new comes at the expense of the old and its associated companies and jobs, creating a win-lose or winner-takes-most economic outcome. Here growth fueled by new-market creation incurs industrial and social disruptions, including very real human costs, as the existing market and its established players and jobs are displaced. Such disruptions produce a trade-off between economic and social good as the world adjusts to the displacement.[18]

With nondisruptive creation, in contrast, the new is achieved without disrupting a preexisting market and its associated compa-

FIGURE 1-1

Two distinct patterns of new market creation and their social implications

Disruptive creation

Economic growth comes *with* social cost of displacement as a new market is created within existing industry boundaries and expands them.

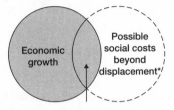

The social cost of displacement occurs as existing market players are being disrupted and made worse off in the process. The overlap is to depict such a trade-off.

Nondisruptive creation

Economic growth comes *without* social cost of displacement as a new market is created outside or beyond existing industry boundaries.

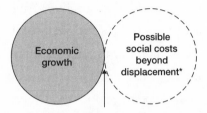

The social cost of displacement does not occur as no market player is being displaced and made clearly worse off in the process. Here, no overlap or trade-off exists.

* These can occur due to negative externalities like air, water, or noise pollution.

nies and jobs. This creates positive-sum growth, because there are no losers, and no market player is made worse off. So growth fueled by nondisruptive creation occurs without incurring any industrial and social disruption and pain, thus helping to bridge the gap between economic and social good.

The distinct economic and social implications of disruptive and nondisruptive creation will be explored and fleshed out in depth in chapter 2. For now, figure 1-1 offers a schematic diagram that depicts the essence of how the social implications of these two patterns of new market creation for growth differ.

As depicted in the figure, *other things being equal* (such as possible other social costs), the difference between disruptive and nondisruptive creation is the social cost of displacement. The figure is just a schematic drawing of this difference that does not in any way represent the real magnitude of economic growth or social costs.

The Need for a Common
Understanding and Theory

If nondisruptive creation is all around us and produces economic growth without incurring social costs, why has it been largely hidden in the world of innovation? And why is it that even companies that achieve nondisruptive creation often call themselves disruptive? After all, wouldn't you want your innovation to be known as nondisruptive if that's what it is? Wouldn't you want to let the world know that the market-creating innovation you unlocked was putting no one out of work, harming no industry or company? All while creating new jobs and growth, and thus helping to bridge the gap between economic and social good. As the book *Contagious*, by the Wharton professor Jonah Berger, reveals, things that reflect positively on a company have social currency and inspire people to share them.[19] Nondisruptive creation largely meets that criterion. So why were companies forfeiting the opportunity to leverage this strategic insight?

Our curiosity piqued, we started to dig down to understand the cause and why disruption has captured the world's imagination and become a near-blanket term for innovation. Consider this quote from John Hicks, the British winner of the Nobel Memorial Prize in Economic Sciences: "Our theories, regarded as tools of analysis, are blinkers. . . . Or it may be politer to say that they are rays of light, which illuminate a part of the target, leaving the rest in the dark. As we use them, we avert our eyes from things that may be relevant."[20]

Established ideas and words lean heavily on us all. They give direction and meaning and wire our brains to be attuned to things. Studies have consistently found that what we look for determines what we see and register. Our assumptions and language direct our subconscious and create path dependency in what is brought to the foreground of our attention and what recedes to the background.

As Hicks suggests, the theories we hold are one of the predominant bases for the assumptions we harbor. They become the mental model or lens through which we look at the world. They shape our perception. Perception is the process by which we detect and interpret environmental stimuli. What makes human perception so pertinent is that, as Hicks notes, we do not simply take in the stimuli in our environment. We go beyond what is present and tend to pay selective attention to those aspects of the environment that are consistent with and support our held theories—and we tend to unconsciously ignore, overlook, or downplay elements that are inconsistent with them. Our brains, in effect, use our mental concepts to modulate and determine what we see.

So if you hold the simple theory that Starbucks is the only coffee worth drinking (as quite a few people do), even if you drive through a crowded city, you'll most likely notice most Starbucks shops that you pass (thinking, *Wow, there's another Starbucks!*) and yet hardly register other coffee shops. Your theory that Starbucks is good will keep you alert to see it *even when* you aren't looking to get a cup of coffee. That's how gripping our theories and beliefs are. The more entrenched a theory is in our mental model, the more dominant its effect is on our perception.

Applying this insight to the field of innovation, we can understand how the compelling and long-standing framing on new-market creation—starting with Schumpeter's notion of creative destruction and segueing into the pervasive idea of disruption—shines light on an important phenomenon that has stood the test of time but also induces a form of bounded rationality that triggers us to interpret reality and keep our focus on identifying and perceiving market-creating innovation through the disruptive lens.

If all you have is a hammer, as the saying goes, everything starts to look like a nail. So instances of nondisruptive creation tend to slide to the background of our attention. And we may even mentally classify them as disruptive. Even if the idea of nondisruptive creation exists in our mental space, unless it is clearly defined and named and explicitly recognized as important, it won't come to the foreground of our thinking and action. We have had neither a common understanding of the concept nor a theory or language system with which to challenge and broaden our conventional framing on the innovation of new markets, which has been shaped by the idea of disruption and creative destruction. We believe that this is a key reason why the idea of nondisruptive creation has been hidden in the world of innovation, even though it has always existed.

Broadening Our View of Innovation and Growth

In today's world, innovation is a must for any firm that wants to achieve sustainable growth. And it's what all companies and countries know they must create to build a prosperous future. In 2018, the distinguished economist Paul Romer won the Nobel Memorial Prize in Economic Sciences for his research that effectively modeled the impact of innovation on economic growth.[21]

While innovation in general is important for economic growth, market-creating innovation in particular is at its heart. It has been the foundation of brand-new industries and the creation of breakthrough products and services.[22]

Look back fifty years. Few poor people in developing countries thought of going to a bank to finance a microbusiness, because they knew they couldn't get a loan without steady employment or a prior credit history. The situation changed when Grameen Bank pioneered the microfinance industry, some forty years ago. Likewise, even people who could have afforded a cruise could not imagine enjoying one about six decades ago, because it was unknown then. The cruise tourism industry was created just around fifty years ago. Similarly, few could imagine taking a trip into space then. But now we are witnessing the development of the space tourism industry by pioneers such as Virgin Galactic, SpaceX, and Blue Origin. Even someone shopping online at Amazon or in a major supermarket has many more choices at a far lower cost than a king of France enjoyed in his day.

These are just a few illustrations of how both nondisruptive and disruptive creations have always been at work in history, continually expanding the industry universe through the creation and re-creation of markets. Both are compelling, complementary approaches to new-market creation for growth with different roles to play in creating brand-new industries and re-creating and expanding existing ones.

By explicitly recognizing and including nondisruptive creation in our conversation on innovation, we can fully tap into its distinctive strength. And with a broadened view of innovation that embraces both kinds of creation, we can see, explore, and capture potential growth opportunities far more widely.

From Blue Ocean Strategy to Nondisruptive Creation

How did we get here? How did we come to explore and understand nondisruptive creation and its impact? In a nutshell, our insight into the concept began when our research in the field of strategy crossed over to that of innovation. Here's how that happened.

More than thirty years ago, in the mid-1980s, we started our research journey in the field of strategy. At the time, the overriding focus in that field was on how to compete in existing industries. To succeed, organizations were urged to analyze those industries and build competitive advantages to beat their rivals. This view of strategy is important and works well when industries are attractive. But in the mid to late 1980s, the world was lurching into a new industrial reality. A slew of global competitors began penetrating the US and world economies. Shrinking profit margins, rising costs, stagnant or declining sales, and market-share battles hit industries as never before. That was when America's Rust Belt came into being, as entire communities found their industrial base wiped out by the surge in global competition, which was only just starting.

These observations raised some questions in our minds. Should strategy continue to focus on competing in existing industries when they were becoming increasingly overcrowded and unattractive? Couldn't strategy also be about how to create new markets to avoid such intense competition? If so, what would it take to create them for strong and profitable growth?

In search of answers to these questions, we studied 150 strategic moves of new-market creation, spanning more than thirty industries and more than a hundred years. The results culminated in our 2005 book, *Blue Ocean Strategy*, which laid out two distinct patterns of strategy: market-competing and market-creating. We called the former "red ocean strategy," because competition in existing industries was increasingly cutthroat and bloody. We called the latter "blue ocean strategy," because markets yet to be created are wide and open like the blue ocean.[23]

As *Blue Ocean Strategy* resonated across the globe, people and organizations shifted their focus from "What is blue ocean strategy?" to "How can we apply its theory and tools to turn red oceans into blue ones?" *Blue Ocean Shift,* our 2017 sequel to *Blue Ocean Strategy,* addressed this issue.[24]

As the energy around blue oceans grew, a question repeatedly popped up from practitioners, academics, and consultants working in the field of innovation. While they asked the question in various ways, it was basically about how blue ocean strategy differs from creative destruction, disruption, or disruptive innovation.

To address that question, we reexamined our blue ocean data from the innovation angle and saw cases such as Novo Nordisk's insulin pen, which significantly displaced existing insulin-market offerings just as Apple's iPhone largely displaced the existing feature-phone industry. These companies re-created existing industries and grew quickly as their innovative offerings significantly displaced the offerings of incumbents. Indeed, their innovation moves were cases of disruptive creation as we have previously defined it. But cases like these were few in our blue ocean data: although they were created *within* existing industry boundaries, almost all blue oceans were created *across* them.

Think of Cirque du Soleil, which created new market space across the existing boundaries of circus and theater. Although it pulled a degree of share from both circuses and theater, generating a measure of disruption, it did not significantly displace either of them as it opened up a big new market space. When a new market is created across, rather than within, existing industry boundaries, a blend of disruptive and nondisruptive growth occurs, but without destruction or full displacement of any existing industry.

We found that unlike creative destruction or disruption as it is widely understood and used in business practice, disruptive innovation has few conceptual commonalities with blue ocean. For example, the iPhone, one of our blue ocean cases, did not innovate the industry with inferior technology from the low-end fringe markets. On the contrary, it did so with superior technology from the high end. Its innovation process was inconsistent with that depicted by Christensen's disruptive innovation, just as Novo Nordisk's insulin pen was. Moreover, blue ocean strategy aims to explain how an organization can achieve growth by creating, not competing. Hence it is more about new-market creation and growth. In contrast, Christensen's disruptive innovation *initially* aimed to explain why industry leaders fail owing to low-end disrupters. Christensen has stated that it is more about the competitive response to disruption than about growth.[25]

Our examination of the blue ocean data also revealed something else very interesting. We saw that among the cases that had been added to our original database over time, a few of them, such as the Square Reader, Compte-Nickel, and the Indian Premier League, triggered no disruption or displacement whatsoever. As we'll detail later in this book, Compte-Nickel created a brand-new market for the unbanked people of France, while the Indian Premier League created an entirely new industry—cricketainment— beyond the bounds of the cricket and sports industries. Unlike the cases of partial displacement (almost all blue ocean cases belong to this category), the few examples in our blue ocean database that involved *no* displacement greatly intrigued us, raising the following research questions.

What is the identity of an innovation that creates a new market without destroying or disrupting an existing one? Could its existence be trivial and hence inconsequential for the existing theory and practice of innovation? But if it has existed across time with some significance, why has it been largely overlooked in the world of innovation and growth? What are its implications for business and society, now and in the future? If it can play a critical role in bridging economic and social good, and shed light on how business can achieve growth and be a beneficial force, is there a process or an approach by which we can conceive and realize it in a systematic way?

These questions inspired us and motivated our research on nondisruptive creation. In conducting it, we went back in time to collect historical and current cases of nondisruptive creation across the for-profit, nonprofit, and public sectors. As we did so, we built a growing new database on nondisruptive creation and the managerial actions involved in it. To include ethnographic elements, we gathered and analyzed written corporate materials, analysts' reports, and publicly available interviews and speeches by the players behind moves that we had come to think of as nondisruptive creation. We also held private conversations with some of them.

Our goal was to discover the common pattern across nondisruptive creation and the shared process and factors leading to their realization. We also used existing cases of blue ocean and disruptive creation for our analyses to contrast with those of nondisruptive creation. We wanted to discern the key differences among these three forms of new-market creation. We examined both convergence among nondisruptive creation moves and divergence among different forms of new-market creation to cross-check and confirm our findings.

As presented in table 1-3, our research showed that nondisruptive creation is a concept distinct from both disruptive creation and blue ocean strategy, with a correspondingly distinct impact on growth. While disruptive creation generates new markets *within* existing industry boundaries, resulting in a high level of disruptive growth, blue ocean strategy creates new markets *across* existing industry boundaries, producing a mix of disruptive and nondisruptive growth. In comparison, nondisruptive creation stands apart, because it creates new markets *outside* existing industry boundaries and generates mostly nondisruptive growth.[26]

TABLE 1-3

Disruptive creation versus blue ocean strategy versus nondisruptive creation

Disruptive creation	Blue ocean strategy	Nondisruptive creation
New markets are created *within* existing industry boundaries	New markets are created *across* existing industry boundaries	New markets are created *outside* existing industry boundaries
All or lots of demand in existing markets is shifted to new ones	Demand created is partly brand new and partly drawn from existing markets	All or most demand created is brand new
Generates significant disruptive growth	Generates a blend of disruptive and nondisruptive growth	Generates mostly nondisruptive growth

As the table shows, with disruptive creation on one end of the innovation spectrum and nondisruptive creation on the other end, blue ocean strategy can be seen as a blend of the two, falling in the middle. Given that ample written materials already exist on blue ocean strategy, our focus here is on nondisruptive creation—the overshadowed and unexplored innovation path. To bring out and fully appreciate its distinctive identity, pattern, and impact, we contrast it with disruptive creation, on the opposite end of the innovation spectrum.

The Future Is Ours to Create

In this book, we have two objectives. First, we aim to show why broadening the existing view of innovation and growth by including nondisruptive creation is of paramount importance today and will be even more so in the future. Toward this aim, we discuss the dis-

tinctive strengths of nondisruptive creation and how it allows organizations to be a force for good while being an important source of
their growth. Second, we aim to show how you can generate nondisruptive creation, by laying out the building blocks for identifying,
acting on, and capturing nondisruptive opportunities and by outlining areas ripe for nondisruptive creation that you can seize.

Here is what you can expect in the chapters ahead. Chapter 2
expands on the impact that nondisruptive creation has on economic growth and society and assesses it in comparison with the
impact of disruptive creation.

Chapter 3 tackles the important issue of why nondisruptive creation should matter to you at the organizational level. We explore
its four distinctive sources of business advantage vis-à-vis disruption
from the vantage point of internal stakeholders, external stakeholders, new entrants, and incumbents. We then discuss its relevance
across industries—including in one of the most competitive and
highly regulated industries in the world—and its profitable growth
impact at the corporate level.

Chapter 4 lays out our case for why nondisruptive creation is not
only an important concept, but likely to grow in importance in the
future. We identify two key emerging forces confronting organizations across the globe: the unleashing of smart machines and
new technologies in the fourth industrial revolution, and the rising
demand for stakeholder capitalism. We explore how those forces
affect the future economic and social value of nondisruptive creation, not only to organizations but to governments, as they strive
to manage the dynamic balance among growth, jobs, and social
stability.

Chapter 5 wraps up the first part of our book by pulling it all
together and presenting a growth model of market-creating innovation that will allow you to act with intent in your innovation efforts.

The model lays out the three innovation paths to new-market creation, what leads to each, and how they generate different types of growth—disruptive or nondisruptive or a blend of the two—so that you can be purposeful in your innovation efforts.

With the significance of nondisruptive creation explored and established, the second part of this book shifts gears and addresses how to realize it.

Chapter 6 lays out the three underlying perspectives that unite successful nondisruptive creators. These perspectives—which revolve around perceptions of agency and environment, technology, and the source of creativity—guide and inform the thought process and conversations of nondisruptive creators and the culture they foster as they conceive and realize their innovations. These perspectives serve as a compass for the process and actions involved in conceiving and realizing a nondisruptive opportunity.

With this compass in mind, chapters 7 through 9 describe the building blocks, and their associated analytic tools, for putting nondisruptive creation into action. Specifically, chapter 7 explores the first building block: how to identify a nondisruptive opportunity, assess its market potential, and frame it in a way that makes it attainable.

Chapter 8 addresses the second building block: how to find a way to unlock the opportunity. Here we introduce the assumption-implication analysis, which provides a structured way for you to unearth and articulate the existing assumptions that have blocked the nondisruptive opportunity, draw the business implications of those assumptions, and challenge and reframe them to find a way to unlock the opportunity. We also outline the challenges you can expect from other people at this stage so that you won't be thrown by them and will stay the course.

Chapter 9 addresses the third and last building block: how to realize the nondisruptive opportunity. Here we provide a framework that shows the three enablers of nondisruptive creation and how they can be creatively leveraged to capture the opportunity in a high-impact, low-cost way. We discuss why having a "could" rather than a "should" mindset is a powerful tool for arriving at the right business model and understanding how to create quick, iterative feedback loops for adjustment and optimization. The chapter concludes with a competence-confidence map that allows you to assess whether you are on the path to succeed, both in the marketplace and with your people, in realizing nondisruptive creation.

Chapter 10 outlines areas ripe for nondisruptive creation and growth that you can explore so that we can all learn to build a better world together.

Chapter Two

The Economic and Social Impact of Nondisruptive Creation

C onsider these examples: Netflix versus Blockbuster, Amazon versus booksellers and Main Street retailers, Uber versus taxis, and, going back in time, airplanes versus transatlantic ocean liners. Although these examples are disparate and cut across various industries and time, they have three key factors in common. First, they're all cases of disruptive creation. Read articles, opinions, executive musings, or investor analysis about them, and the word you'll encounter most often to describe these dynamics is *disruption*. Second, they all reflect a clear win-lose situation. And third, they all impose painful adjustment costs on society, even as consumers win. Let's explore this.

On the positive side, consumers and purchasers win big time. That's why people gravitate to the disruptive offering, be it Netflix, Amazon, Uber, or any other. For a product or a service to disrupt, it must deliver a leap in value (typically underscored by a new business model), or the industry wouldn't be thrown into disarray, and purchasers, whether they be businesses or consumers, would see no reason to shift from the incumbent offering to the new one.

Think of how Netflix disrupted Blockbuster. With no late charges; a low, flat monthly fee for unlimited films; and movies delivered straight to your home—via mail and now via online streaming (which allows us to watch films with no advance planning or need to run to the store)—Netflix's innovative business model offered consumers irresistible value over Blockbuster and other independent video-rental stores. And consumers—more than 200 million of them—rewarded it with their wallets, spurring Netflix's strong growth and high valuation.

Or take Amazon, which initially disrupted booksellers and, as we know, is today disrupting Main Street retail. Ask consumers or businesses why they choose Amazon, and you'll get a flood of positive comments: "I love that I can always find the book or item that I want." "The direct customer reviews and ratings are great and helpful." "I can see what related products I might need or want to try given my interests." "Checkout is fast and a cinch." "I can order everything straight from my couch, and delivery is getting amazingly fast." A woman in the audience at one of our talks said, "When it comes to Christmas, I tell my kids if it's not on Amazon, it doesn't exist." Amazon could hardly have made a more powerful statement as testimony for its leap in value. In that woman's mind, there is no other store. Or no other store can hold a candle to Amazon in her view.

In economic terms, we can say that the consumer surplus delivered by the disrupter is high, and society's resources are allocated where they are deemed to be better used. The leap in consumer surplus is why so many of us shop at Amazon, take Uber, are addicted to snapping digital photos, and binge-watch Netflix. We feel that they better our lives. It's also why disruptive creations tend to grow industries as the compelling value unlocked by their innovative business models draws all new people to their offerings who weren't purchasers of incumbents' products or services and inspires previous customers of the incumbent industry to use the disruptive product or service more frequently. For example, more people watch Netflix than rented DVDs from Blockbuster, and clearly more people take digital photos than ever took photos with film—just as far more people cross the ocean in planes than ever did on ocean liners, and with greater frequency.

The leap in consumer surplus also explains why disruptive creation occurs from both the low and the high ends, as we discussed in chapter 1.[1] That's because consumer surplus is a function *not* of price per se but of the greater value delivered, where value is the nonprice performance or benefit obtained at a given price. When the benefit delivered for the price is of an order of magnitude greater than the old benefit delivered for the old price, disruption tends to occur. The incandescent light bulb was high-priced, yet its immense superiority in terms of reliability, safety, convenience, and health led to a leap in consumer surplus, resulting in near total displacement of the kerosene lamp. Similarly, Apple's iPhone was expensive, but it offered a leap in nonprice performance that easily wowed users with its cool design, access to the internet, and touch-screen interface, creating consumer surplus an order of magnitude greater than what had previously existed. The iPhone rapidly displaced both the feature phone and nascent smartphone offerings as customers lined up for hours to purchase one.

Whether disruptive creation occurs from the high or the low end, however, here growth is achieved in a win-lose way. The disrupter wins, but its success comes at the direct expense of existing players and markets. Which brings us to the second commonality: disruptive creation imposes a clear trade-off between winners and losers, the extent of which depends on the degree of displacement. In some cases, it's a one-wins, one-hundred-lose situation. That's because the leap in consumer surplus provided by the disrupter can nearly wipe out the existing industry and its incumbent players, as airplanes pretty much did to ocean liners. Reduced demand for the old translates into reduced earnings for incumbent players and the existing market.

For example, Amazon didn't merely displace Borders' 1,200 stores and countless independent booksellers and take a huge chunk out of Barnes & Noble's sales. It is doing the same to Main Street retailers and department stores nationwide. As Amazon has won big time with strong growth, most of these other players have been losing big time with an alarming rate of store and mall closings and bankruptcies across America (already a reality well before Covid hit). Today Amazon accounts for 50 percent of online retail sales in the United States. Likewise, Uber didn't kill or usurp the sales of any one taxi company. Its disruptive move hurt industry revenues across the board in nearly every city it entered. Nationally, receipts from Certify Software show that Uber and other ride-hailing services saw their share of the business-ground-transport market jump from a mere 8 percent in 2014 to more than 70 percent by 2018.

As for Netflix, it has all but wiped out physical video-rental stores, and more and more people have cut their cable subscriptions as well in favor of the company. Blockbuster, once the largest video-rental business in America, has but one store standing today. As for ocean liners, while they once accounted for 100 percent of ocean crossings, today they account for less than 5 percent, with airplanes accounting for 95 percent or more of a now far larger transatlantic industry. Steve Jobs proclaimed that the iPhone would reinvent the phone industry, and indeed, it became one of the best-selling products in history, turning Apple into one of the world's most valuable publicly traded companies. But the aftermath was the failure of giants—Nokia, Sony-Ericsson, Motorola, and BlackBerry—and the shuttering of their cell-phone businesses.

To summarize the economic impact of disruptive creation: it offers a leap in consumer surplus for purchasers and all users. Society's resources are allocated where, in economic terms, they are better used. And it can awaken surviving companies and push them to up their game for the benefit of consumers. Although demand shifts from the losers to the winner, disruptive creation tends to buttress the aggregate growth of the economy far beyond the shift over time. The total demand generated by disruption minus the demand transferred from the disrupted players and industry is generally positive. Restated, net growth over time can generally be expected.

While the disrupter's win is hailed in the press, and purchasers and investors flock to it, this win-lose approach triggers the third commonality: painful adjustment costs for society, including various levels of hurt and hardship. The euphoria and glamour that surround disruptive creation tend to largely blind us to these, yet there they stand: a loss of existing jobs and often rounds of layoffs, lowered wages and hurt communities, and knowledge, skills, and plant and equipment often rendered significantly reduced in value, if not made obsolete. Even when the economic costs involved in such disruptions are small relative to the overall economy, the social costs incurred can be extremely large for the people, companies, and communities that are affected owing to the human sufferings of losers and the impaired harmony and trust among winners and losers, all of which have destabilizing effects on society.

In New York City, for example, Uber's largest US market, the company has had a huge impact on the livelihood of taxi drivers and medallion owners. Long seen as a retirement ticket, taxi medallions, which grant their owners the right to operate a taxi and to lease it to someone else, have plunged in value from more than $1 million to as little as $175,000 since the appearance of Uber and other ride-hailing services. Taxi drivers' earnings have nosedived by as much as 40 percent; many drivers must now work double shifts just to survive. Bankruptcies, foreclosures, evictions, and even suicides have resulted: eight New York City taxi drivers have taken their own lives because of mounting financial woes as their taxi earnings have cratered. The New York Taxi Workers Alliance is now on the alert for indications of depression among drivers. These negative aftershocks are felt not only in New York but also in major cities across the world where Uber and similar services have entered. The same disruptive force that has enriched consumers with its leap in value is small comfort for the people who've been hurt in the process.

Or consider digital photography's disruption of Kodak. Kodak's workforce plummeted from a high of 86,000 employees to fewer than 2,000. Many thousands of people lost their jobs, while their career-long knowledge and skills took a large hit in value. For the region around Rochester, New York, where the company was based and for generations was its largest employer, the decline meant not only the loss of all those good-paying, great-benefits jobs but also a huge negative impact on vendors, retailers, service firms, and non-profit organizations, as people's lost incomes diminished their spending and local investments. This loss was arguably large enough to hurt the city community.

With Amazon's disruption of bookstores, more than 30,000 jobs were lost when Borders shut its doors, not to mention all the jobs lost as scores of independent bookstores went out of business. Barnes &

Noble finally buckled too, adding tens of thousands more lost jobs. But the effect goes beyond the loss of jobs. Bookstores are part of the fabric of communities, a sentimental place where culture, history, and neighborhoods come together. When a town loses a bookstore, many feel that the community has lost a part of its soul.

The human costs of Amazon's disruption of retail are equally if not more pronounced: tens to hundreds of thousands of lost jobs, not to mention the visual effect of forlorn, boarded-up stores, which subtly wears on people's psyches and tarnishes the vibrancy of a community. Retail jobs may not be glamorous, but they provide livelihoods for millions of people.

These social adjustment costs are triggered by the transfer of demand—and with it, jobs—from the established order to the disrupter. It's what we call the "zone of transfer" that sets off the social pain. The greater the full-on disruption, the greater this zone of transfer will be, and the greater the short-term to medium-term hardship imposed on society as it absorbs the pain and slowly adjusts to the new reality. Which is to say that disruption unleashes not only positive effects, but also negative and very real human effects on the economy.

Although the people who are let go may find work in another industry, that's not guaranteed—especially when they're in rural communities where local jobs were scarce to begin with. Of course, disruption triggers new growth and jobs, because people must be hired to fulfill the new aggregate consumption it unlocks. For example, Amazon's disruption of booksellers and retail has led to estimates of as many as 900,000 jobs lost; but at the same time, Amazon's workforce, excluding the people it effectively acquired when it purchased Whole Foods, climbed from 200,000 to 800,000 when Covid hit. Amazon's net positive impact on jobs has been growing steadily, which is a plus for the economy and to some extent softens the blow. That does not mean, however, that Amazon jobs are located where the old jobs were lost, or that they rest on the same skills and knowledge as those of the people let go. So those who were let go can still be left reeling. There's also no guarantee that disrupters' surging growth will necessarily lead to a net addition of jobs in the economy, because their business models are increasingly technology-centric.

At its peak, in 2004, Blockbuster had 60,000 employees and 9,000 stores with revenues of $5.9 billion. Netflix has markedly grown demand and the size of the industry, pulling in revenues of more than $20 billion in 2019. Yet it employs fewer than 8,000 people. So even though Netflix created compelling economic growth for the economy, the company, and its shareholders, its tech-centric business model relies on some 80 percent fewer employees—a net loss of more than 50,000 jobs.

These social adjustment costs and spillover effects are negative externalities. Negative externalities arise as market creation and market destruction, and with them, job creation and job destruction, are inextricably linked under disruptive creation. Which is to say that the impact on employment of disruptive creation is also net, not gross. It's a function of the total jobs generated by disruption minus the total jobs lost by the disrupted players and industry. That's a key reason why, as we'll discuss in chapter 3, disruptive creation often triggers a backlash from external stakeholders, with social interest groups, government agencies, and nonprofit associations more inclined to lobby against, clamp down on, rein in, or tax the disrupter in an effort to minimize the carnage wrought by disruption's zone of transfer.

In essence, disruptive creation produces a win-lose situation even though at the macro level the new consumption it unlocks in the long run creates aggregate growth—not simply the transfer of demand from the old to the new. Here the disrupter inadvertently produces human and social costs in the short and medium terms to generate private profits, imposing—all else being equal—a trade-off on society as it performs its unique role of re-creating industries from within for growth. In the case that an industry has a pronounced negative side effect on the environment or the well-being of people, this trade-off, however, may be small relative to the overall benefit to society of disrupting and displacing that industry. That would be the case, for example, if coal-fired power plants were disrupted and displaced by clean, reliable, and cost-effective energy sources. The greater social good to be weighed and considered would be elimination of the industry's deleterious side effects, such as pollution, vis-à-vis social adjustment costs through disruption. The greater an industry's harmful side effects to be displaced, the greater would-be disruptive creation's net positive impact on society. With such an industry, disruptive creation may be the needed path to innovation and growth for the greater social good.

When Market-Creating Innovation Yields a Positive-Sum Outcome

Here is where nondisruptive creation breaks from disruption. By effectively disentangling market creation from market destruction, it allows organizations to grow with little to no social pain imposed. All else being equal, you can think of it as a positive-sum approach to innovation—as opposed to the win-lose nature of disruptive creation—which we find not only promising but a much-needed complement to disruption in the world of innovation. Let's explore the similarities and the differences.

First, like disruption, nondisruptive creation delivers compelling value for buyers, whether they are consumers or businesses.

It positively changes our lives. That's why we purchase or use the product or service and the new market materializes. Unless it delivers compelling value, as disruptive creation does, the new market will not take off. That's a prerequisite, just as it is for disruption.

When the nondisruptive move of Sesame Street was created, for example, it offered parents a brand-new opportunity in the comfort of their own homes for their preschool children to learn colors, shapes, the alphabet, and important skills such as listening. It also afforded parents a brief reprieve during which to take a peaceful shower or attend to other household matters. And by mixing fantasy with reality and adding songs and silliness, the colorful, lovable Muppets (a cross between "marionettes" and "puppets") won over children, too, as they developed a foundation for early school.

With 3M's Post-it Notes, people needed little more than to receive a single Post-it on a document to become quickly addicted to this nondisruptive offering. The little yellow note did not move when people shuffled papers or an unexpected breeze entered the room. And yet when they went to remove the securely adhered note, it came off as though it had never been stuck. It's not unusual for first-time users of Post-its to stick one to a surface, pull it off, examine the paper front and back, and then restick it and repeat in small amazement. We know because we did it ourselves. Post-it Notes fast became indispensable in offices and homes for reminders and notes to colleagues, families, and oneself.

Whether it is Music: Not Impossible for the deaf ("I am finally able to experience music like everyone else!"); Viagra for men (after years of struggle, the struggle is gone); the Square Reader for small businesses ("At last, I too can offer credit card payments"); life coaching; or the Star Walk app for any of us to gaze up at the night sky and know the stars and planets we are looking at ("There's

Orion! I could never identify the constellations before!")—each one offers compelling value to buyers and users.

But, in contrast to disruptive creation, growth here is achieved without displacing existing industries or incumbent players. Here there is no evident loser. And precisely because of that, there are also minimal to no painful adjustment costs imposed on society. Which is to say that nondisruptive creation has a positive impact on growth and jobs from the start.

Kickstarter, for example, saw that there were literally thousands upon thousands of young (and old) creatives who had wildly imaginative projects they dreamed to create but who lacked the capital to realize them. You know the type—the often hip-dressed waiters and waitresses who work in quirky small restaurants or coffee bars with cool, Zen-like names. The ideas they dreamed of realizing could be something as eccentric as sending an anonymous hand-written letter to every single person in a town, all mailed on the same day, to see people's reactions when they discovered that every-one they ran into had received one. "What! You mean you received one too?! How bizarre!" "Who wrote this? What could this mean? Why our town?" It doesn't take much to imagine that these letters might instantly captivate an entire community and become a story shared till people went to their graves—one of those do-you-remember-the-time-when stories that define our lives.

A project like that actually got funded on Kickstarter with, like most creative works, no financial return. Most creatives don't aim to generate an ROI. They create first and foremost to simply realize an artistic vision in their minds. So it should come as no surprise that Kickstarter's online crowdfunding platform did not displace or take away even a tiny share of existing equity investors' or venture capitalists' profit, growth, or investment opportunities and didn't eat into the existing finance industry. And because backers receive no monetary incentives on Kickstarter—only cool merch or other recognition such as a shout-out on the creative's website—a new set of investors emerged: people who care about creative work and helping others realize their dreams.

Hailed after its launch as one of *Time* magazine's "50 best inventions" of the year, Kickstarter won but it created few if any losers. Within three years of its launch, it became profitable, and in its first decade it raised a staggering $4.3 billion for projects supported on its platform, successfully funding more than 160,000 ideas that by all accounts would have gone unrealized otherwise. According to a study at the University of Pennsylvania, Kickstarter estimates that more than 300,000 part-time and full-time jobs were created by its projects, along with 8,800 new companies and nonprofits, generating more than $5.3 billion in direct economic impact for those creators and their communities. No one lost a job because of Kickstarter, and no company went out of business because of it. It helped the artistic community flourish without unleashing hurt or painful adjustment costs on society. It's pretty much a win all around.

Or take the nondisruptive move of Space Force, created in December 2019. Although that year was a highly contentious time in US politics, Space Force's compelling value to US security and the American way of life gained it bipartisan support: it passed in both the Democrat-led House and the Republican-led Senate, and its creation was written into law.

Space Force is the first new military service created by the US government in seventy years. It challenges the age-old adage that the sky is the limit. Its strategic scope—the stars, the planets, the moons, and beyond—begins where Earth's atmosphere ends. It was created to respond to new and emerging strategic challenges.

When people reflect on space and its mysteries and challenges, images of a future akin to *Star Wars* or *Lost in Space* often come to mind. We wonder whether there could be life beyond: Is there water? Is there any form of oxygen or vegetation? How can we overcome the lack of gravity so that we could actually walk on another planet without having to wear some restrictive, heavy space suit?

Most of us don't realize how much of our everyday lives and our security have rapidly become tied to space. Satellites now provide the backbone of our daily lives. The GPS in our cars, ATMs, hospitals, power grids, banks, gas pumps, traffic lights—all rely on satellites circling the earth to operate. So do missile warning systems, cell phones, and the cloud that stores all your beloved photos. Whether it's disaster relief, humanitarian assistance, or deterrence and security, space is enabling it. We just don't see that.

Cyberattacks and the jamming or kinetic destruction of satellites are growing strategic challenges. They can severely impact nations' and corporations' security and very viability and thus people's lives. When satellites are jammed and rescue missions cannot access required information, lives are lost and national security is at risk. What's more, microsatellites can create a debris field that travels at 17,000 miles an hour. At that speed, a piece of metal the size of a coin can be weaponized. And cyberattacks are accelerating rapidly at the corporate level. With more than 50 percent of them targeting American companies, their damage to the US economy is estimated at some $100 billion annually. This costs an estimated 500,000 jobs each year as revenues are stolen and truncated by cyberattacks that take down sites, infiltrate corporate networks, and wipe or steal data, trade secrets, and IP.

With the many advances in technology, and private companies such as Elon Musk's SpaceX building reusable rockets to take civilians into space as well as working to create a new economy and community on Mars, space has never been more important or more potentially contentious across nations.

Space Force's unique aim is to ensure security in space, keep satellites safe and operational, and deter conflict by developing technology and promoting space diplomacy to address the unique, rapidly evolving opportunities and threats space provides. Currently, the only existing treaty on outer space says that no nation may have a nuclear weapon in space. Otherwise, space can be thought of as the outer world's wild, wild West.

To achieve its mission, Space Force is focusing on growing a unique professional cadre of space thinkers, concept developers, writers, and technologists who understand how the seemingly unending void, in which there is no up or down, left or right, borders or place to hide, changes everything. Space, in short, requires a very different skill set involving different multi-orbit architectures, different training, and different partnerships, tactics, techniques, and procedures.

Space Force does not displace any existing private companies or industries or any preexisting military units. Although it was only recently established, its budget for 2022 is estimated to be about $20 billion, with a projected increase of $2.6 billion over the next five years as it builds out its ranks and new jobs are created to meet the many and growing challenges it faces. A nondisruptive move of this magnitude and complexity takes time to fully realize, but it promises huge potential for economic growth and jobs.

Disruptive versus Nondisruptive Creation

Table 2-1 presents the gist of our discussions so far, outlining the key defining features of disruptive and nondisruptive creations at what economists refer to as the micro, the meso, and the macro levels. While the micro level focuses on individual organizations,

TABLE 2-1

Disruptive versus nondisruptive creation

	Disruptive creation	Nondisruptive creation
Micro-level consequences	Generates growth through the displacement and expansion of existing market space.	Generates growth through the creation of new market space beyond existing industries.
Meso-level consequences	Produces a win-lose outcome.	Produces a positive-sum outcome.
	Winners: the disrupter and consumers.	Winners: the nondisruptive creator and consumers.
	Losers: disrupted organizations and their employees.	Losers: no evident loser.
Macro-level consequences	Incurs social adjustment costs due to shuttered organizations, lost jobs, and hurt communities.	Incurs no evident social adjustment cost as there is no displacement.
	Yields disruptive growth where the growth comes with social pain. But the *net* gain in economic growth over time is positive.	Yields nondisruptive growth where the growth comes without social pain. The gain in economic growth and employment is positive from the start.

the meso and macro levels deal with groups or their interactions and the economy or society, respectively.

The Precessional or Secondary Effect

When bees travel from flower to flower to collect pollen, their mission is to make honey. Yet in the process, as we know, pollen sticks to their spindly little legs and is dusted on other flowers as they buzz about, allowing yet more flowers to bloom and grow. Buckminster Fuller, a renowned American systems theorist, called this the "precessional effect."[2]

No business or organization exists in isolation. Innovation and growth trigger precessional effects—or, in economic terms, secondary effects—on third parties. So it is with both disruptive and nondisruptive creation. Beyond the direct impacts noted in the table, both have precessional or secondary effects on their ecosystems or value networks, and these effects can loom large.

Amazon's disruption of booksellers and retail, for example, led to growth in the ecosystem of package delivery as Amazon partners with hundreds of third-party courier companies nationwide that hire and manage their own fleets of trucks and vans to handle the company's last-mile-delivery needs. There's also Amazon's secondary effect on the packaging materials industry, with so many goods, once purchased in stores, now packed individually by Amazon and mailed directly to people's homes. While Amazon knocked off thousands of booksellers and retailers, it has also had a secondary impact on growth by forcing still-standing players to rethink and improve their operations and by spurring innovation in others. The same can be said of nondisruptive creation. Think, for example, of the secondary effects on outside companies, ranging from aerospace technology to robotics, AI, and astrophysics, that Space Force's nondisruptive move is likely to trigger. It will probably also spur space-related private companies' innovation, along with efficiency in design, manufacturing, and operations.

But here there is a difference worth noting. Amazon's secondary impacts on the ecosystems of packaging materials and package delivery come in conjunction with the decline in retail real estate values that Amazon indirectly triggered. That's because ancillary industries attached to a disrupted industry tend to experience disruptive effects as well (as retail real estate has), while the disrupter's new business model bolsters the growth of third parties (such as package delivery and packaging businesses) in its new ecosystem.

As a result, a *net* indirect impact, either positive or negative, is to be expected since few industries stand alone without supporting business ecosystems.

When it comes to nondisruptive creation, however, the secondary impacts are more akin to Buckminster Fuller's precessional effect of bees, because nondisruptive creation tends to have primarily positive indirect effects and few if any third-party losers. That's because few if any ancillary industry players or existing ecosystems would be displaced under nondisruptive creation. So whatever secondary impact it has on growth and jobs will tend to be positive from the start.

Whether the long-run positive impacts of disruptive creation on growth and employment are greater or lesser than those of nondisruptive creation depends on a host of factors, such as the nature of the innovation, its effect on people's way of life over time, and the trajectory of industrial development. Hence it is nearly impossible to assess the impacts of disruptive and nondisruptive creations in relative terms. We do know, however, that social costs can be expected in at least the initial period of disruptive creation, whereas such costs tend to be largely absent with nondisruptive creation.

Driven by Hope or Fear?

Have you ever noticed how much in business is about aggression and fear? We all dislike such behavior and emotion, because they fill us with anxiety and make us feel that we are under threat and may be marginalized or destroyed if we don't strike first. It's a scarcity-based view of the world. While the world needs less of that behavior and that emotion, we have been conditioned to pursue them to achieve success and even to better the world.

What if we could instead shift our frame of thinking from fear to hope, from a scarcity-based mindset to one of abundance? Thinking that we can create and grow without disrupting or destroying others stands on the ground of hope that creation can be positive-sum rather than a destructive, fear-based win-lose game.[3] It's an abundance-based view of the world that nondisruptive creation's distinctive role in creating brand-new markets outside existing industries allows us to start moving toward.

Nevertheless, we all know that in reality, fear and hope are equally compelling motivators for making people act and getting things done. Fear invoked by a competitive challenge or a threat like "disrupt or die" is a strong motivator for an organization to act. However, the hope of making a positive-sum contribution to both business and society is an equally strong mobilizer. So it's fair to say that nondisruptive creation is based on a view of the world that is complementary to that of disruptive creation.

In the next chapter, we go beyond the impact that nondisruptive creation has on economic growth and society and explore the important question of why nondisruptive creation should matter to you as an organization, whether you are an entrant or an incumbent.

Chapter Three

The Four Sources
of Business Advantage

When thinking about innovation and growth, the economic and social impact of your approach is not all that matters. What also matters is an organization's ability to successfully implement it. Disruptive creation has an advantage in that the industry to be disrupted provides a clear target of a known market size and deals with a known need for which people have demonstrated a willingness to pay. Nondisruptive creation may appear more challenging precisely because it occurs outside existing market boundaries, where there is no such target or known need for which people have demonstrated a willingness to pay.

In the second part of this book, which is all about learning to identify and capture a nondisruptive opportunity in a more systematic way, we'll show how to overcome these challenges. There, we will outline not only a different type of target—one that will give your innovation efforts for creating a nondisruptive market clear direction and focus—but also a way to assess its commercial potential and realize it.

That said, nondisruptive creation has its own organizational and business advantages, which, we have found, stem from four sources. While the four sources of advantages may not all apply in every case of nondisruptive creation, the majority will.

The four sources of advantage include:

- The ability of an industry entrant, whether a startup or an established organization, to bypass big incumbent players with significant resources and reach in their innovation efforts.

- The ability of an incumbent to respond to a full-on disruptive threat without confrontation. Nondisruptive creation opens a nonconfrontational path to seize new growth when challenged by a disrupter.

- The responses of internal stakeholders to your innovation efforts. Nondisruptive creation is emotionally and politically easier for incumbents' internal stakeholders to get behind.

- The responses of external stakeholders to your innovation efforts. While disruptive creation tends to increase conflicts with social interest groups and governments, nondisruptive creation largely sidesteps these challenges.

Figure 3-1 shows the four advantages of nondisruptive creation vis-à-vis disruption. Let's dive into each.

FIGURE 3-1

The four sources of advantages

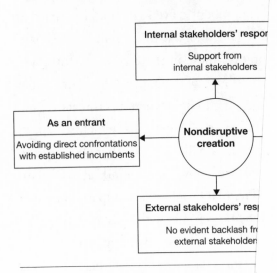

wher
start
try a
confi
cial,
almo
indus

Co
disru
scribe
tially
its off
start.
receiv
refuse
bulk f
Movie
and ga
costs o

Not
the U
agreem
for unl
block i
costing
It woul
than fiv
had ma
Stacy S
Over
of prici

Avoiding Direct Confro
Established Incu

A long love affair has gone on betwee
tive creation. Consider Mark Zuckerb
book: "Move fast and break things." V
alike are excited by stories of David t
the emotional pull of such stories is st
can be.

Not surprisingly, the hope of many
ing industry and become the next un
pitch businesses that aim to destroy th
industry. Unlike established organiza
easy to align around and embrace di

it comes to execution. But when a company—whether a
p or an established organization—sets out to disrupt an indus-
d eat the lunch of incumbent players, it should prepare to
nt well-entrenched organizations with deep network, finan-
nd marketing resources, which, in the case of startups, will
certainly tower over those of their own. And any target
ry is more than likely going to fight when it is threatened.
sider the recent experience of MoviePass, which set out to
the movie theater industry with a service that allowed sub-
s to watch a set number of movies per month at a substan-
wer cost than that of regular tickets. The company launched
ing in San Francisco and was met with resistance from the
lthough some 19,000 city residents happily signed up to
one 2D movie a day for a flat monthly fee, theater owners
to honor the tickets, which the company had purchased in
m a third-party supplier. Theater owners appreciated that
ass was in effect disintermediating theaters and moviegoers
ning market power, leaving theaters to bear the investment
real estate and films.
ntil three years later did the AMC movie theater chain in
ted States agree to cooperate with MoviePass. But the
nt required MoviePass to charge a flat monthly fee of $45
nited movies. At that price, AMC effectively put a road-
front of MoviePass's disruptive move. With movie tickets
8 or $9 at the time, the subscription fee set a high hurdle.
make sense only for people committed to seeing more
movies a month. Not surprisingly, in two years MoviePass
aged to sign up only 20,000 members. The founders,
kes and Hamet Watt, sought help and hired a new CEO.
he next two years, MoviePass went through several rounds
g changes with varying subscription conditions in an

attempt to disrupt the market and reach its growth targets. Its strategic objective was clear: "get big fast" to achieve economies of scale and the needed bargaining power vis-à-vis incumbents. The case MoviePass made to theaters was that its subscription service would provide them with additional revenue by filling their empty seats. In return, the company hoped to get ticket discounts and a share of concession revenues from theaters. The bigger its subscription base, however, the bigger its bargaining power would be in negotiations with the incumbents, and the incumbents understood that.

MoviePass's decisive disruptive strike came in August 2017. It launched an all-you-can-watch subscription for the unbelievable price of $9.99 a month—essentially the cost of one adult ticket. Moviegoers were thrilled. By April 2018, MoviePass's subscriber base had skyrocketed to about 3 million. Theater owners did not take this lightly and set out to fight. AMC, the largest US movie chain, held a press conference that criticized the move and engaged in a monthslong public feud with the company. It then announced its intention to shut its theater doors to MoviePass subscribers, truncating the service's reach. By June 2018, AMC had announced its own subscription service, called AMC Stubs A-List. As that subscription service became popular and successful, other big theater chains, such as Regal and Cinemark, followed suit.

MoviePass burned through cash, incurring monthly losses in the millions to subsidize its low price, as its bargaining power against incumbents melted away. With the biggest chains now offering attractive terms that it couldn't match, such as early ticket purchases, MoviePass ran out of money and was forced to shut down its subscription service in September 2019.

The popular press may make it seem that disruptive moves by nimble and clever startups frequently outsmart dull and conventional incumbents, but the truth is that incumbents often prevail.

The failures of would-be disruptive startups tend to remain hidden unless they are very high profile, like that of MoviePass.

Furthermore, in many industries, buyers have sunk costs in using an existing industry's product or service, which a disrupter may have to account for in getting buyers to switch. If people are fairly satisfied with the offering they currently use, they're unlikely to be looking for a replacement. So converting sales to a disruptive offering—even with a superior solution—may be far slower than the disrupter predicts. That has been a key challenge for solar-paneled roofs, which set out to disrupt the traditional roof industry. Yes, they promise lower to nonexistent heating and electricity costs, not to mention the emotional satisfaction and status of being (and being seen as) an environmentally conscious citizen. But steep sunk costs in their existing roofs have created substantial inertia among homeowners, so far limiting solar's disruptive capability.

The question is: Do you really want to directly confront well-entrenched incumbents and the potentially significant sunk costs of buyers? That's certainly one way to go. And it may be a good way under certain market conditions, such as when your disruptive move offers a big increase in value on several dimensions. That was the case for transatlantic air travel, which offered a leap in speed, convenience, and glamorous aura over ocean liners, and for email (free, fast, and instantaneous across the globe) versus snail mail. Indeed, many unicorns were born that way. But bear in mind that there is an alternative way to innovate and grow without disrupting. Opportunities for nondisruptive creation loom just as large, and any company—startup or incumbent—would be wise not to over-look them. As we'll show, unicorns are created that way too.

Consider the experience of Square and GoPro, vastly different from that of MoviePass. They are good examples of companies that avoided direct confrontation with or backlash from existing players by launching nondisruptive new markets outside existing industry boundaries that unlocked growth with no destruction.

Founded by Jack Dorsey and Jim McKelvey, Square saw an untapped opportunity to create a nondisruptive market outside the boundaries of the US credit card industry. While Americans could use their credit cards with large and medium-sized merchants, they couldn't charge purchases from most small merchants, self-employed individuals, or microbusinesses such as farmers' market vendors, food trucks, and pop-up shops, for whom existing point-of-sale technologies for processing transactions were too costly to install and complicated to maintain, and the processing fees were too high.

Square also saw that people would be thrilled to use credit or debit cards for small transactions that are typically handled by cash or check—which banks, too, would love to do away with, because they are essentially a nuisance courtesy offered to clients. Having discerned this vast untapped opportunity outside the credit card industry, Square set out to seize it. Its solution was a mobile payment system through a small plastic device called a Square Reader, which you simply plug into your mobile phone. The Square Reader is easy to use and easy to carry, and you pay only when you use the device, making it attractive for small businesses, pop-up shops, and even individual transactions, such as for babysitters, ice cream trucks, and handymen.

Square's nondisruptive move created, but it did not destroy. It caused remarkably little if any disruption to existing merchants and their credit card providers. As a result, Square was able to grow quickly into a billion-dollar company without facing any real back-lash or fight from established players. As we all learn as kids, if you don't tread on others, others are rarely motivated to tread on you. Life reflects back what we send outward. Square's cofounder Jim

McKelvey wrote a thoughtful article titled "Good Entrepreneurs Don't Set Out to Disrupt" in the May 2020 issue of *Harvard Business Review*, which pretty much says it all.[1]

Like Square, GoPro created a nondisruptive market—the action-camera industry—and with it a brand-new opportunity for sports enthusiasts to film their own live-action adventures from a first-person perspective. They could film themselves as they were engaged in surfing a large wave or skydiving, and yet be fully present in the moment because their hands were free.

Consider the startling difference. For the first time, instead of needing a third party to shoot them in action, sports enthusiasts could capture what they experienced and saw from their own vantage point. Getting an existing digital camera wet meant damaging if not breaking it, whereas GoPro's cameras are waterproof and made to work when fully wet. Unlike existing digital cameras, which are meant to be held, they are meant to be attached—to a helmet, a wrist, a headband, a snowboard—so that your full body can perform the sport while the camera is recording your live-action experience. And whereas digital cameras require a fair level of care so that they aren't dropped or banged, GoPro's are built to handle all that and more, because sports are intensive.

As the nondisruptive action-camera industry grew, GoPro rose to become a billion-dollar company. Did established DSLR camera players, with their deep pockets and brand names, attack GoPro, try to stop it, or fight back? No. GoPro's rise did not eat into their industry. No Goliath felt vulnerable or challenged on the bottom line. Nor did buyers have to overcome sunk costs or switching costs. After more than a decade of growth and success, GoPro, like all companies, has had its share of ups and downs. But the brand is still synonymous with, and the dominant player in, the nondisruptive action-camera industry it pioneered. And cell phones haven't been able to disrupt and displace it as they have the camera industry.

If disruption drives your thinking, ask yourself what nondisruptive opportunities you might be missing. That question is particularly important if the disruptive move you are contemplating does not confer a significant leap in value along several dimensions in comparison with incumbents.[2] By setting aside the preconception that disruption is the way, and thinking in terms of nondisruptive creation, you become a sharper observer of nondisruptive opportunities lurking on the horizon (or right in front of you) that would sidestep rather than take on established players, providing new and previously unseen avenues for economic growth. Remember, no industry player is happy when its reason for being is under attack.

An Effective Way to Respond
to Full-On Disruption

Nondisruptive creation can also open a way to respond effectively to full-on disruption. To see this opportunity, however, you must be open to it. You can't be locked into thinking that disruption can be countered only with disruption. Consider: many people today see the world as a sort of global village. Leaving aside the pause for Covid, international travel has skyrocketed over the years. Our own business school, INSEAD, has students who fly in from more than fifty countries to study on one of our three campuses in France, Singapore, or Abu Dhabi. And they can swing (travel) between those campuses during their matriculating year.

The era of international travel began with the golden age of transatlantic oceangoing, which started in the mid nineteenth century with ocean liners. Passenger liners flourished for a hundred years. At first, crossing the Atlantic took more than two weeks. But by the 1860s the introduction of iron hulls, compound steam engines, and screw propulsion had reduced crossing times to about eight or nine days. No longer limited by the technical constraints of wood armatures, liners also increased substantially in size, with a capacity of 1,500 passengers, up from 200 earlier. The number of liner services across the Atlantic (and across the world) grew, and the length of a transatlantic crossing eventually shrank to five days. Demand for the passenger liner industry continued to grow.

The British company Cunard was a leader in the industry. Cunard transported millions of immigrants from Europe to the United States around the turn of the nineteenth century, and its vessels played an important role in transporting troops to battle, wounded warriors home, and refugees to safety during the two world wars and other conflicts. Winston Churchill said that the Cunard line's efforts sped up the end of World War II by nearly a year. Cunard's ocean liners also carried diplomats, CEOs, and royalty from one continent to another. By the end of WWII, Cunard had emerged as the largest Atlantic passenger line, operating twelve ships to the United States and Canada as it captured the flourishing North Atlantic travel market in the first postwar decade.

But that golden age came to an end when commercial air flights disrupted the entire industry. In 1958 Pan American Airways started its transatlantic flight service between New York and Paris with a Boeing 707. The 707 was the first commercially successful jet; it soon dominated passenger air transport in the 1960s and ushered in the jet age. In 1957, 1 million passengers crossed the Atlantic Ocean by sea. By 1965, that figure had fallen to 650,000. More telling, the sea-to-air ratio was 14:86 in 1965. That is, for every fourteen people who crossed the Atlantic by sea, eighty-six chose to cross by plane.

They had good reason. Ocean liners simply could not match the speed and convenience of the jet age. Instead of five days to cross the Atlantic, air travel took half a day. Flights were regular and often compared with sea travel. And Pan American, the world's number one airline at the time, epitomized glamour and sophistication. Pan Am stewardesses were a cultural icon. Royalty, world leaders, and Hollywood stars flew with Pan Am.

The writing was on the wall. Cunard saw no way its ocean liners could match or beat the speed and convenience offered by transatlantic air travel.

What to do?

The company's first instinct was to match this disruptive move. It reasoned that more than one could play this game. So Cunard set out to enter the airline industry and preempt the market disruption with its own disruption before the entire ocean liner industry was displaced. In March 1960, Cunard bought a 60 percent equity stake in a new airline, Eagle Airways, and rebranded it as Cunard Eagle. Cunard Eagle was the first independent airline in the UK to be awarded a license by the newly created Air Transport Licensing Board (ATLB). The airlines retaliated. Cunard's leading British competitor, the state-owned British Overseas Airways Corporation (BOAC), immediately appealed to the minister of aviation and got Cunard Eagle's license revoked. BOAC was not about to share the highly traveled North Atlantic air route. With Cunard's disruptive move thwarted, the ATLB threw Cunard Eagle a small bone: it gave the airline permission to fly the far-less-traveled UK-Bermuda-Nassau and then Miami routes. Not long after, Cunard exited the industry.

After its failed disruptive move, Cunard pivoted and made a nondisruptive, market-creating move by innovating "luxury vacationing at sea," ushering in the modern cruise industry. Up to that point, ocean liners, like airlines and cars, were principally viewed as a mode of transportation from point A to point B. Now the ocean liner would no longer be a means to an end. Rather, the voyage itself would be the end. It would be a vacation. People would take cruises more for pleasure and star-studded entertainment than to be transported between two places. Cunard's "one-class" cruising ensured that all passengers—regardless of the staterooms or berths they booked—enjoyed the same activities, live performances, food, services, and other amenities.

Cunard's nondisruptive creation allowed it to escape the disruptive force of airlines that destroyed other ocean liners. The company today is part of Carnival Corporation, and the cruise tourism industry it pioneered some sixty years ago has generated about $150 billion in revenues and more than a million jobs. This has opened up vast business opportunities for others as well—a good outcome for all—business, economy, and people.

Or take the French postal service, La Poste. The digital disruption of email and texting hit La Poste hard. Over the past decade, the number of letters La Poste delivers dropped by nearly 50 percent, and it continues to fall. But with emails and texts delivered instantly and free, La Poste saw no viable disruptive counterpunch to match the threat. What it did see was a way to leverage its extensive presence in every corner of France, and the natural link between the French and their postal workers, to make a nondisruptive market-creating move called Veiller Sur Mes Parents (VSMP) or Watch Over My Parents.

In France, a growing social problem is the loneliness of elders. Adult children increasingly live and work in cities and towns far from their aging parents' homes. The distance between them, compounded by the busyness of young people's lives, all too often leaves the elderly alone with long gaps between visits, making their isolation, and thus their emotional well-being and health, an issue of rising social concern.

La Poste's launch of VSMP stepped in to address this unsolved and growing social problem. According to a survey commissioned by the postal service, French citizens rank mail carriers among their favorite figures encountered in daily life, second only to bakers. VSMP builds on that trust and natural familiarity. It enlists mail carriers to provide the elderly with a relaxed form of human connection and conversation and a way to check that they are okay.

For less than forty euros a month, family members can arrange for seniors to receive weekly home visits from their postal worker. After a visit, the postal worker uses an app to inform the adult children if their parent is well and whether assistance with groceries, home repairs, outings, or other needs is required. Seniors can also sign up on their own. Since the introduction of VSMP, La Poste has expanded on its nondisruptive move: postal workers also deliver supplies from shops, basic prescriptions, library books, and hot meals to elderly customers, though they are paid for by local councils. VSMP has provided a nondisruptive new market for the growing number of elderly people living alone and in need of human connection, and a new revenue stream for La Poste. It's a pioneering move that sheds light on the types of opportunities that can open up for us when we think beyond disruptive creation.

The lesson: next time you confront a disruptive threat, don't view your strategic options as limited to disrupting back and fighting fire with fire. Of course, that's one way to meet the challenge of disruption, and it may work for you. But remember that it's not the only way. Instead, like Cunard and La Poste, broaden your thinking to embrace and think deeply about nondisruptive creation as well.

Nondisruptive creation may provide a more viable and creative response, especially when the threat you face is as acute as jet air travel was to ocean liners or as email and text messages have been to letter writing. And as with Cunard and La Poste, opportunities for nondisruptive creation often come from leveraging and building on assets and capabilities your organization already has.

Support from Internal Stakeholders

On March 13, 2012, the *Encyclopaedia Britannica* (EB) announced the final edition of the oldest, continuously published, reference source in the English language. Once the defining mark of an educated household, the *Britannica* had become a shadow of its former self. The cause, as we know, was the digital distribution of encyclopedic knowledge—think Wikipedia—which disrupted and displaced the global market for hardbound encyclopedias.

What many don't know, however, is that EB was no stranger to the digital distribution of encyclopedic knowledge. It had ventured into that realm a decade before Wikipedia even existed, creating a new unit, the Advanced Technology Group, which had seen the writing on the wall as PCs started to take off and internet adoption was creeping into existence. By as early as 1994, EB had launched the Britannica CD-ROM encyclopedia for PCs and a website, eb.com, for institutions such as universities and libraries that had already purchased its hardbound encyclopedias. Yet by 1995 its sales had tumbled 50 percent from their high. And by 1996 the company had been sold for a fraction of its earlier value.

What went wrong?

All companies want to innovate. As the existing markets they play in are challenged by disruptive threats, most of them appreciate that growth will rest on going beyond incremental innovation and making market-innovation moves. But established companies face high execution hurdles with internal stakeholders—employees, directors, executives, managers, and investors—when innovating in the marketplace means displacing their existing business and the revenues that go with it.[3]

Rightly or wrongly, when faced with disrupting their existing business, people are naturally inclined to use their direct and indirect influence to undermine their own company's disruptive move, even if that undercuts the company's long-term future. This is especially true for those whose interests, expertise, and beliefs are anchored in the existing business model. This inclination can lead to subversive and unhealthy corporate behaviors. It's also demotivating.

That leaves top management with a quandary: how fast should we destroy our known, profitable business with a new business model in which the economics work differently, and which may not even be profitable in the short to medium term? Executives are hard-pressed. They don't relish the short-term stress or organizational upheaval that such a change can create for the company and its financials. For this reason, people from the top down are often inclined to ultimately work to protect the current business model.

In EB's case, no one doubted that its most valuable asset was its approximately 2,000 well-trained door-to-door salespeople, who drove the organization. Its full-time salesforce was rumored to close on one of every three leads, which is even more astonishing given that its encyclopedias cost $1,500 apiece and provided an additional, reoccurring revenue stream from the yearly updated edition. So when EB set out to commercialize its CD-ROM version to counter the disruption PCs foretold, its salespeople understandably pushed back. They were already being pinched by Microsoft, which a year earlier had launched a CD-ROM encyclopedia, Encarta, at $295. The idea that their own company would further chip away at their commissions by launching a disruptive alternative didn't sit well.

Management faced a tough choice. It could launch the CD-ROM version using a different distribution method and a lower price to counter Microsoft's disruptive move. But that would create internal conflict and the likely departure of some salespeople, along with the steep revenues they brought in, in exchange for the uncertain revenues that the CD-ROM version might deliver. Estimates were that seven to ten CD-ROM versions would have to be sold to equal the income from one hardbound sale. Not surprisingly, EB's leaders saw that they had much more to lose than to gain by moving full steam ahead on disruption. To keep the salesforce motivated and not jeopardize the company's lifeblood revenue, they decided to launch the CD-ROM as a free bonus for people who bought the hardbound edition. If a potential buyer wanted the CD-ROM version on its own, it would still be sold for near to full price of the hardbound one. But at that steep price, and with PCs taking off, not even the bundling could slow down the disruption. By the time Britannica lowered the price of its CD-ROM version to fit the market, it was too late.

As Britannica's story, like those of Kodak and Nokia, illustrates, it is far easier to advise that your existing business be disrupted than it is to actually do it. The internal organizational hurdles are steep: fear of certain revenue losses for uncertain disruptive gains—but also fear of losing one's job or status by moving away from their existing competence—can prompt managers to undermine disruptive projects.[4] As for leaders, few are eager to confront challenging and often unmanageable conflicts among internal stakeholders and to pay painful organizational costs.

As one top executive of a global oil giant put it, "We have 50,000-plus people working in the crude oil business, from exploration to refinery to distribution and retail sales. And then we have a small fraction of that working on renewables to disrupt and displace oil's lock on energy. But when you have 50,000-plus people behind oil, there is a lot of power and influence that is reluctant to kill their bread and butter on their watch. No one wants to dig their own grave. So naturally there is a human incentive to passively undermine alternative energy initiatives in the company, even though they're important. Sometimes that just means slapping the initiatives with lots of corporate overhead, which quickly kills their profit prospects, slows or shuts the resource spigot, or inspires the best to want off the initiative. In the end, you set out to disrupt the market, and then the human enters the equation. You need very strong leadership to pull that off, and I've seen few companies that have what it takes when disrupting the market means killing a business that works well and pulls in solid revenues."

The point about strong leadership is important here. It's one thing when you aim to disrupt the market and that threatens to displace someone else's business. But it's a completely different story when that means disrupting your own business. That gets personal superfast. It's like changing the engine while driving—scary and very hard. Netflix is among the few companies that successfully disrupted a market along with its core business and cash cow. But look who is at the helm. The founder and the central driver of its disruptive corporate culture, Reed Hastings. Few large companies have that. That lends credibility and natural ability to push through organizational hurdles that, frankly, most professionally hired managers and executives lack.

Look no further than the conflict between the former CEO of Blockbuster, John Antioco, and its key activist shareholder, Carl Icahn. After initially dismissing Netflix as an online niche player, Antioco and his team soon saw the need to make a significant shift to online. They launched Blockbuster Online in 2004 and followed it up in November 2006 with Total Access. Under Total Access, people could rent a DVD online and return it to any Blockbuster store in exchange for a free new movie of their choice. (This was before video streaming was a technological reality.) Total Access quickly gained traction, doubling its subscription membership in only six weeks. Blockbuster was now adding more subscribers than Netflix, rattling its rival.

Before Total Access was fully executed, however, the conflict between Antioco and Icahn erupted. In 2007, Icahn—provoked by the steep losses involved in the online project, which were damaging the bottom line—engineered Antioco's resignation after a salary dispute. Blockbuster store owners also lobbied hard against the company's online moves, in fear of losing current sales. As we know, Blockbuster went bankrupt. Even as its disruptive counterpunch was gaining steam, internal hurdles derailed its execution.

It should be clear by now that none of these companies were run by foolish people with their heads in the sand. These scenarios reveal what makes disruptive creation particularly hard when it means displacing a company's existing business, whether in a spinoff or not.[5]

Here is where a broader understanding of nondisruptive creation provides a real advantage. For established companies, nondisruptive creation opens a much less threatening path to growth and market innovation than disruption does. For one thing, it doesn't directly challenge the existing order or the people who make their livelihoods based on it, so it's easier for leaders to implement. For another, it doesn't mean killing existing revenues that Wall Street, investors, and employees all look to and depend on. Few executives are inclined to upset investors or go through the short-term nightmare of displacing their own business. Established companies can better manage their organizational politics, the anxieties of their people, and the expectations of shareholders if there's no question of killing or replacing existing revenues.[6]

Take 3M. More than a hundred years old, with $30 billion in annual sales, 3M produces adhesives, abrasives, and laminates among other products. To foster organic growth, it puts great emphasis on R&D. In its R&D labs, Spencer Silver, a scientist who researched adhesives, discovered something peculiar called a microsphere— an adhesive that sticks lightly to surfaces but doesn't bond tightly to them, making it easy to peel off. Silver was at a loss for a use for his discovery, because it was neither strong nor tough—the marks of a good adhesive. Lacking a commercial opportunity, his discovery was left sitting in the lab.

Enter Art Fry, a new scientist at 3M. Fry observed that paper used as a bookmark fell out of the book. He experienced the problem at church choir practice, where his hymn notes regularly fell out of his songbook. Having learned of Silver's discovery, Fry saw a brand-new opportunity that went far beyond bookmarks. If Silver's microspheres could be put on paper, the paper could be attached and removed easily without leaving any residue. You could leave notes in books, on colleagues' doors to remind them of a meeting or on a report requesting them to review it, or on your desk as a reminder to make that difficult call you had been putting off for weeks. They'd stick well and then peel off with no wear and tear. This was a nondisruptive opportunity that wouldn't displace any established industry or players outside *or* inside 3M.

When Fry explained his idea to Silver, the two became a team. They encountered the questions and scrutiny that typically come with almost all innovations: after all, a nonadhesive adhesive was essentially an oxymoron. What they didn't experience, however, was emotional pushback, political undermining, or organizational hurdles erected to subtly or not so subtly trip up the project, even as they worked through the two-steps-forward, one-step-back testing and refining phase. Instead, the atmosphere at 3M was emotionally and politically supportive. It was clear that if it succeeded, this market-creating innovation wouldn't displace any existing business. It would only add revenues and jobs.

Silver's lab director, Geoff Nicholson, jumped in to help. He started passing out samples of the sticky notes to senior executives' secretaries, who almost instantly adored them. When the sticky notes didn't catch on in an initial test market because people couldn't actually try the product before purchasing it, Nicholson and the division vice president went to the chair of the board and the CEO to get funding for a sampling blitz in a test market. They packed a trailer with samples and drove to another city to pass out notes to every potential customer. And the rest is history. The nondisruptive market for Post-it Notes was born, and with it a brand-new growth engine for 3M.

Like Post-it Notes, Viagra was a nondisruptive creation. Pfizer created the blue pill that does away with impotence for men. Before Viagra (generically known as sildenafil), erectile dysfunction (ED) was an unaddressed and unspoken problem for men pretty much around the world. Upon its launch, Viagra quickly became a household name, and a brand-new nondisruptive market was opened.

Yet Viagra didn't start out as a drug to address ED. Surprisingly, it was developed as a treatment for high blood pressure. But development trials showed that it didn't consistently work. Then something happened. At the end of a clinical trial involving Welsh mine workers, the researchers asked if the men had noticed anything else while taking the drug. It turned out that the drug had a titillating side effect. One man confessed to getting more erections during the night, and the other mine workers smilingly agreed. A light bulb went off.

Pfizer's managers were surprised and cautious about what they learned. Sildenafil already had an air of failure at the company, owing to the poor blood-pressure trials. But the researchers made a strong case for this brand-new market opportunity and won £150,000 to do an impotence study. The study confirmed what the mine workers had experienced: the drug worked to remedy ED. Even more telling, the men who participated in the clinical tests refused to give back the pills when the trial ended.

Because the marketplace offered no other widely accepted treatment for ED, Viagra promised huge pent-up demand. More than that, it would not displace any of the company's existing drugs; it would only create a new growth engine for the company if it succeeded. So Pfizer's internal stakeholders fully embraced moving forward to create the nondisruptive market.

As is true with any new drug, Pfizer encountered challenges when it set out to commercialize and build the business model for Viagra. How could the stigma be taken out of impotency? Would religious groups take offense at a "sex pill"? Could doctors and experts, who thought of drugs mainly for medical conditions, be sold on the value of a lifestyle drug? But the company did not waver or hedge. Internal resistance was low. No existing unit felt threatened. People felt energized rather than fearful. Although no one could predict just how big the nondisruptive market would be, they knew that solving impotence was deeply important to men, that many men over fifty struggled with it, and that the market offered no viable alternative. Pfizer's scientists, doctors, salespeople, marketers, and management were all-hands-on-deck to make this nondisruptive opportunity work.

Soon after its launch, Viagra became a global phenomenon, making it one of the highest-grossing prescription drugs in Pfizer's portfolio. As of 2020, it had generated more than $30 billion in sales for the company.

Now stop for a moment and imagine: if disruption can get people's backs up, lead to short-term organizational upheaval, and often create challenging financial decisions about when to slay the bird in the hand to capture the bird in the bush, wouldn't we all do well to open our opportunity horizons by more systematically exploring nondisruptive creation? There is a lot of money, opportunity, and impact to be realized in this less threatening form of market-creating innovation, in both advanced economies and less-developed nations, as the cases of 3M, Pfizer, Grameen Bank, and other companies we discuss in this book reveal. We've seen that by framing their market-creating efforts in a broader context that explicitly embraces both disruptive and nondisruptive creation, established companies can better manage their organizational politics and the anxieties of their people in pursuing market creation—and typically achieve better buy-in in the process.

No Evident Backlash from External Stakeholders

This last advantage stems from the responses of the people or groups outside the organization that are nonetheless affected by the organization's market-innovation moves. They extend beyond relevant industry players to include society, government, nonprofit associations and agencies, and even the media.

By its very nature of being creative but not disruptive, nondisruptive creation largely avoids triggering negative backlash from external stakeholders. That doesn't mean that it skirts standard regulatory scrutiny and actions. It doesn't. The Food and Drug Administration, for example, stepped in and mandated that 23andMe make its direct-to-consumer genetic testing information much clearer to consumers and clarify that its genetic tests aren't meant to diagnose a disease. In the same way, the FDA mandated that Pfizer specify potential negative side effects of Viagra and pass all standard regulatory hurdles for its drug approval. Any new market-creating innovation, nondisruptive or not, can and should expect that.[7]

Where disruptive creation differs, however, is that it is more apt to spark external stakeholder backlash. Because it displaces existing players and often cleverly maneuvers around industry rules and regulations, it is more likely to cause social interest groups, government agencies, and nonprofit associations to lobby against, clamp down on, rein in, or tax the disrupter in an effort to minimize the carnage and level the playing field. All of which can rapidly consume the resources and time of the disrupter, lift its cost structure, and constrict the growth of its market-creating innovation. Often the players that are at risk of being disrupted lobby hard behind the scenes to get other external stakeholders to discourage and block the disruptive challenger.

Take Tada, the Korean ride-hailing service, which was forced by government mandate to shut down. It had launched its service in October 2018, using spacious eleven-seat vans that could be hailed with an app. It was explosively popular among users who were frustrated by the often reckless driving and rude manners of taxi drivers. As the earnings of Korean taxi drivers plunged, several drivers committed suicide, sounding an alarm in the social health sector. Hostile street protests and strong demonstrations broke out, with the nation's 300,000 licensed taxi drivers behind them.

With its far-reaching implications for both business and society, the controversy attracted a wide variety of business and community groups, along with the government, legal institutions, media, and interested academic circles. The central point of debate was the contribution to the economy of Tada's mobility innovation versus the cost of social conflicts and the disruption it caused.

Tada's service was built on an exceptional clause in Korea's Passenger Transportation Service Act, which allowed a vehicle with eleven to fifteen seats to be paid for transportation services even if the driver didn't have a taxi license. While Tada's service aligned with the law, the exceptional clause had originally been created to support group tours for the tourism industry, not van-size taxis.

The cries were so loud against Tada and its clever use of the legal exception that in April 2020 the Korean National Assembly amended the law with the specific aim of banning Tada-like taxi businesses. Tada fought hard and appealed, but the Constitutional Court ruled against it, stating that the company's service greatly increased social conflict. The amended law would stand and would create a level playing field in the transportation industry.

Another example is Smile Direct Club (SDC), which set out to disrupt the billion-dollar orthodontics industry by leveraging teledentistry and 3D printing of clear teeth aligners. Priced at $1,895 (versus $5,000–$7,000 for regular braces), with a treatment time of six months (versus the standard twenty-four months) and no need for repeated office visits to the orthodontist, SDC's product took off fast. But as the company grew, it found itself facing a barrage of legal attacks that have substantially eaten into management time and company resources. In April 2017, the 18,000-member American Association of Orthodontists filed complaints in thirty-six states alleging that SDC was breaking laws governing the practice of dentistry, arguing that the standard of care in essence requires the services of traditional in-office orthodontics. The American Dental Association passed a resolution "strongly discouraging" the public from using services like SDC, even as it's received lots of positive customer reviews. And in May 2018, in lieu of a standard audit, an investigator for the enforcement unit of the Dental Board of California (DBC) ordered a raid on SDC's stores in broad daylight, allegedly scaring customers and store employees. The raid was picked up and reported on social media, harming SDC's credibility and image. The company is pursuing legal action against the DBC, arguing that as a state regulatory board controlled by market participants, it was in violation of antitrust law by taking actions without state oversight.

The disruptive moves of Tada and Smile Direct challenged existing industries in which the governing rules had been formulated with existing industry practices and stakeholders in mind. When disrupters creatively leverage regulatory loopholes or challenge industry practices with vastly different business models that undermine the existing industry, they should be prepared for authorities and industry associations to catch on and try to close those regulatory gaps or put forth arguments to block new business models to minimize the disruptive consequences and meet external stakeholders' opposition and complaints. In the case of Amazon, several European countries have come to the rescue of local bookstores by imposing legislative limits on the discounts Amazon may provide.

Because nondisruptive creation doesn't leave social carnage in its wake, it largely sidesteps negative backlash. As it solves brand-new problems or creates brand-new opportunities outside existing industry boundaries, society tends to be open to nondisruptive market innovations—once it understands the offerings and their value. Whether it be Post-it Notes, Music: Not Impossible, the Square Reader, or Sesame Street, GoPro, microfinance, Viagra, or Halloween pet costumes: none of these roused external stakeholders to respond with intense litigious attacks, counter-lobby to truncate and rein in the innovation, or push back as jobs in their community came under threat.

Think Nondisruptive Creation Is Not Possible in Your Industry? Think Again

Finance is among the most competitive industries. Companies in this sector tend to hire employees from only the best business schools and only the top graduates from those schools. People in the industry notoriously work long hours and are known to be highly driven and supercompetitive—those in venture capital, investment banking, hedge funds, and private equity as well as in corporate finance, retail, and consumer banking.

Finance also faces increasing regulation and is one of the fields most heavily regulated by the government. New legal requirements for capital, stress tests, transparency, and know-your-client and anti–money laundering regulations are getting more attention. Meanwhile, the global regulatory framework has been fragmenting, forcing financial institutions to contend with numerous, often unfinalized legal requirements whose implications have yet to be fully realized.

Intense competition and steep regulation, such as what the finance industry faces, are among the most common factors that organizations and individuals cite when claiming that nondisruptive creation is "not possible in my industry." They reason that intense competition leaves no innovative stone unturned and that high regulation ties a company's hands behind its back so that it can't act innovatively.

Yet the facts in the highly competitive and highly regulated finance industry do not bear this out. In addition to the multimillion-

and multibillion-dollar nondisruptive industries created by micro-finance, the Square Reader, and Kickstarter, consider a recent nondisruptive creation unlocked by two companies founded by INSEAD graduates.

Every year a growing number of students from across the globe seek to do advanced studies abroad. But in most countries, foreign students cannot easily get a loan to pay for their studies unless they have a local cosigner or a strong credit history or collateral in the country. This poses a significant unaddressed problem for many students: they must either shelve their aspirations or put them off for years as they cobble together the needed funds.

Prodigy Finance, based in the UK, set out to solve this long-unaddressed problem. Its founders learned firsthand at INSEAD how many students had faced this challenge and were forced to postpone admission because of it. As Cameron Stevens, one of the founders of Prodigy, put it, "I thought the hard part was getting into a top business school abroad. That ended up being the easy part. The hard part was getting a loan to cover advanced studies outside your own country. No banks would do it." The solution was a new model for making foreign student loans that wouldn't require a local cosigner or collateral. It also wouldn't rely on a credit history in the country of study, which foreign students don't have.

The company recognized that students who pursue advanced studies abroad are highly motivated. Many seek out the best insti-tutions in higher education, which will lift their career prospects still higher. By assessing foreign students according to their merit—their academic performance and future earning potential—Prodigy can lend to previously "unlendable" foreign students the funds to fulfill their dreams and keep defaults low. Prodigy—along with MPOWER Financing, based in the United States and also founded by INSEAD alumni—are unlocking a new multibillion-dollar nondisruptive market that is producing the next generation of global talent while earning a tidy profit.

The company Compte-Nickel (renamed Nickel in 2018), founded in 2014, saw a wide-open opportunity for nondisruptive creation in France, even though the country has multiple banks in every town. By 2018 BNP, one of France's largest banks, had acquired a 95 percent share of Compte-Nickel for €200 million, and with that Compte-Nickel was renamed. In France, a large number of people are excluded from banks, owing to their financial status. Who are they? People with only intermittent work and unsteady incomes, youths, low-income earners, and the unemployed who depend on others for money: almost 8 percent of the country's population. Yet all these people increasingly need access to a credit card because cash is becoming less and less acceptable even for items as basic as mobile phone service.

Compte-Nickel set out to create a brand-new opportunity for the unbankable people of France. The answer was a "bank in a box." It takes less than ten minutes to set up, using only a resident card and a mobile phone, and requires no proof of income. It's easy, nondiscriminatory, and fast. Here's how it works: Stop by any of the 4,000 news agencies dotting France. Show your ID to get a bright-orange box. Inside, you'll find an International Bank Account Number and a Mastercard debit card that functions internationally, all for just €20. Account management is entirely electronic, via internet banking, online statements, and text messages. For a flat annual fee of €50, customers can withdraw money at any ATM, deposit or withdraw cash at any of the partner news agencies, and send and receive wire transfers. From the moment they get the box, they can start using their credit card and Nickel account. All they have to do is give the news agency the funds they want to start their account with, and bingo—the account is up and running.

Or jump to the African continent and consider the nondisruptive market-creating innovation M-PESA, launched in Kenya in 2007. Previously, Kenya's economy was largely cash-based, and only a small proportion of the population had access to banks, which were located only in the major city centers. But carrying cash made people targets for street robberies and muggings, and cash stashed at home invited regular burglaries. What's more, to take cash back to their families in the villages, as was the custom, people had to spend hard-earned money to ride buses, which too often were stopped by roaming bandits in search of cash. M-PESA changed all that. It stepped in to address a burning but unaddressed problem that was hurting both people and society.

Created by Vodafone's Kenyan subsidiary, Safaricom, M-PESA provides people with a safe, secure, and affordable way to send, receive, and store money; pay bills; and deposit salaries, all via their mobile phone accounts. To deposit or withdraw money, a user simply goes to any of the thousands of local kiosks—the type that sell cigarettes and chewing gum—across the country and hands cash to the kiosk representative, who registers the amount in a ledger and on the user's mobile phone account. The funds can be transferred to anyone in Kenya with the push of a button, and the recipient will receive a notification saying who sent the money. Money can be withdrawn the same way: the user goes to a kiosk, shows the representative the account balance, and asks for the sum needed. Fees are charged on a transaction basis.

The creation of M-PESA unlocked huge and burgeoning new demand. The service now has more than 35 million active customers and almost 400,000 agents operating across seven countries. In 2020, those customers conducted more than 11 billion transactions—an average of some 500 transactions every second. Nearly 50 percent of Kenya's GDP—about 3.6 trillion Kenyan shillings, or €29 billion—was processed through M-PESA in 2017. The nondisruptive market it created now accounts for more than 30 percent of Safaricom's overall revenues.

If in one of the most intensely competitive and stringently regulated industries in both developed and developing economies, all these companies saw an opportunity to create a new market where once none existed, what is possible for you? We need to realize just how broad and achievable nondisruptive creation is, not just in finance, but for all of us.

The Performance Consequences of Nondisruptive Creation

Even after forty years, despite the technology-obsessed world we live in today, 3M still sells some $1 billion worth of its Post-it Notes every year. Viagra, a decade after its patent expired, still brings Pfizer some $500 million annually. And Safaricom's M-PESA generates nearly $800 million in revenue annually. But it's not just these nondisruptive creations that have had a profound impact on their company's profitable growth. The nondisruptive creations of the Square Reader, GoPro, Prodigy, and Cunard have done something similar.

As organizations try to strengthen their market positions today while creating and spurring growth for tomorrow, pursuing nondisruptive opportunities can unlock multimillion- and multibillion-dollar new markets sometimes as big as or even bigger than what their existing offerings bring in.[8] This can be seen in the impact on the Japanese company Park24 as it created a nondisruptive new market in, of all things, car parking in Japan's congested big cities.

Park24 started out as a manufacturer and vendor of "No Parking" signs and parking equipment for car-park owners and managers. But, in search of its next chunk of profitable growth, the company saw an opportunity for nondisruptive creation. An existing but long accepted problem in Japan's highly congested cities was the acute shortage of parking. The streets were narrow and teeming with motor vehicles, bikes, and pedestrians, making on-street parking generally forbidden because it would significantly block traffic. In addition, a scarcity of suitable land made it extremely difficult to find a parcel large enough for a car park—and even if one was found, the price was typically prohibitive. It was just not a lucrative business to pursue, despite the huge unaddressed demand.

Park24 conceptualized innovating a market that would make parking as available as the convenience stores found on every corner. To realize this brand-new concept of convenience-store-like parking—think little parking lots ensconced throughout the city— the company scouted out small plots of idle land scattered across the busiest cities and found a wealth of essentially unused patches of land near popular destinations. Sometimes these were located between buildings and were too small to be used for any obvious purposes: the owners had inherited them along with bigger pieces of property and did not know what to do with them. In other cases, an owner might be sitting on idle land until the right price was offered.

Park24's nondisruptive business involved renting these odd plots of land, allowing their owners to turn idle property into revenue generators without lifting a finger, and using the land to create what became known as Park24 Times sites, which typically provided four to seven slots. The service was fully automated: when a vehicle parked in a space, a pump triggered a moving plate to raise and block the vehicle, which would be lowered and allow the vehicle to exit only after the owner made payment at a kiosk. The automated system made it possible for Park24 to roll out its convenience-store-like parking rapidly, at low cost, with no limits on hours of operation, since no staff was required. To encourage drivers to park for the shortest time needed—to increase turnover and parking opportunities for other drivers—Park24 initially set a flat rate for every twenty minutes. Drivers could park conveniently and safely and be close to their destination.

As the brand power of Times quickly grew, Park24 was able to increase its brand-new car-park market by leveraging not only idle land but also the "idle time" of land. The best locations in town centers were often occupied by major banks or government buildings— facilities that were utilized only on weekdays during business hours. Park24 negotiated with banks and government agencies to rent their idle parking spaces after hours, on weekends, and on bank holidays, greatly expanding Park24 Times' parking spots while turning a cost factor into a revenue generator for those organizations.

Today, Park24 Group is a holding company with annual sales of nearly $3 billion. By addressing a long-standing and accepted problem that nobody thought could be solved, Park24 created a fast-growing, nondisruptive market in Japan. Although parking in the country's major cities is still in very short supply, the number of slots more than quadrupled over ten years, largely thanks to Park24's nondisruptive market of Times parking, which generates more than $1 billion a year.

From "Out There" to "Near Here"

When humans wanted to understand the stars and the cosmos, but our eyes were not keen enough to detect their wonders from afar, the nondisruptive creation called the telescope was conceived. And when we wanted to see the composition of bacteria and viruses so that clues to disease cures could be found, the nondisruptive creation called the microscope was born. Nondisruptive creation can be as "out there" as Elon Musk's ambition to create the first community on Mars. It can also be far more basic—like Park24 Times. Whether the nondisruptive opportunities are out there or near here, they all fall outside existing industry boundaries. What we know by now, according to the historical data, is that nondisruptive creation is a compelling source of profitable growth.

In the next chapter, we'll discuss two key emerging trends cutting across the global economy and why they are likely to place a growing premium on unlocking nondisruptive creation, now and in the future.

Chapter Four

The Rising Importance
of Nondisruptive Creation

E ver since the Nobel Prize–winning economist Milton Friedman, arguably one of the most influential thought leaders of
the twentieth century, introduced his theory of shareholder
primacy, there has been a presumed trade-off between maximizing
economic gain and social good. Friedman's theory is at the heart of
capitalism as we know it today. He posited that the sole purpose of
a firm is to make money for its shareholders. So long as a business
stays within the rules of the game, not using deception or fraud,
Friedman argued, "there is one and only one social responsibility
of business—to use its resources and engage in activities designed
to increase its profits."[1] Maximizing profit, and thus shareholder
value, provides sufficient social benefit. Social issues beyond that
fall outside the proper scope of the enterprise.

This view has dominated economic thought for the past fifty years. Yet for all the economic benefits it has brought, it is increasingly called into question. The world is waking up to realize that costly negative externalities have been imposed on society and our communities in the pursuit of profit maximization. And society is getting more and more vocal about these externalities, with millennials and Generation Z often leading the charge, demanding that corporations expand their mission beyond profit and that shareholders consider the impact of organizations' actions on the broader stakeholders of society.

Historically, firms have addressed demands for social accountability largely through corporate social responsibility initiatives and practices and charitable giving. Here, however, social good and stakeholder concerns are—for all intents and purposes—effectively a cost function. In other words, they attempt to address stakeholders and social good not in how organizations *make* money but in how they *spend* it.

The weakness in this approach is that economic good and social good are essentially treated as separate. It's a siloed approach. So when economics get tough, those initiatives, not surprisingly, are often pared down or even abandoned. They remain more or less a sideshow to the main event of economic growth. But to suggest that social good should replace economic good as the prime focus of business would be naive. Just focusing on doing social good can't cut it, as much as people may cry out for that. It's practical reality. Without economic success, there can be no money with which to do social good. A growing economy is an economy that generates the vital outcome of wealth, which provides both the resources needed to address social issues and the basis on which jobs are created.

Rather than treating social good and shareholder concerns as separate, it would seem more effective if we work to integrate the two. This would bring us closer to a socially responsible form of capitalism in practice. Indeed, discussions about the need for this are increasing.[2] But although the concepts of stakeholders, stakeholder theory, and stakeholder capitalism have existed for decades, concrete suggestions about how to achieve this in a way that does not stifle corporate growth or profits but rather fosters them have been few and lacking. Nevertheless, many leaders of today are issuing calls for firms to accomplish just that.

To answer these calls, firms are increasingly urged to pursue their strategies in a win-win manner for themselves *and* society. Their innovation strategies for growth are no exception. What, then, is a viable future strategic direction for innovation as a key engine of economic growth if it must play a positive-sum role for society? How can we create an innovation strategy that chips away at the long-standing trade-off between economic growth and social good?

Answering these questions is neither easy nor intuitive. And there are most likely various ways to achieve this goal. However, as we learned in chapter 2, when it comes to the innovation of new markets, nondisruptive creation presents one workable path toward addressing this challenge. Here social good is not a sideshow but is locked into economic good by its very nature of creating without destroying, thus generating nondisruptive growth. In other words, with nondisruptive creation, social good is not achieved in how companies *spend* money but begins to be achieved in the very way they *make* money to thrive and prosper. Instead of compromising economic good, nondisruptive creation brings economic good and social good closer to moving in lockstep.

In the view of some, governmental measures for assessing and enforcing corporate social responsibility are misplaced when they are divorced from business reality. While a distinction needs to be made between *the idea* of stakeholders, stakeholder theory, or stakeholder capitalism and *how* it is realized, such institutionalized measures, rightly or wrongly, become a focus for criticism of the idea itself. What we propose here is a step toward addressing such criticism.

People want to believe that the company they work for not only creates innovative offerings that positively influence people's lives but, in so doing, does not destroy the lives of others. So by social good here, we mean the unique ability of nondisruptive creation to innovate new markets without causing the social harm of shuttered companies, lost jobs, and hurt communities that occurs when market creation comes with market destruction.

The rising importance of breaking this trade-off underscores one of the main reasons we believe that nondisruptive creation is likely to only grow in importance in the future. And why responsible executives cannot afford to ignore it. The other main reason lies in the fourth industrial revolution that is upon us.

The Challenge of the Fourth Industrial Revolution

Although the Industrial Revolution is often thought of as a single continuous event, it can be better understood as four sequential revolutions or paradigm shifts. The first, which began in the late eighteenth century, was propelled by mechanization and steam power. The second, in the nineteenth century, was fostered by mass production, electricity, and the assembly line. The third, which took place in the twentieth century, introduced computers, automation, and information technologies.

The fourth industrial revolution, which we are now experiencing, encompasses the advent and convergence of exponential technologies—from artificial intelligence and smart machines to robotics, blockchain, and virtual reality—that are already affecting the way we live. Whenever you query Siri, for example, to find a restaurant's address, or ask Alexa to call your mom, you are using AI, whether you are conscious of it or not.

All these new technologies are on track to trigger leaps in productivity greater than we have ever seen before. And with these leaps in productivity will come increasingly lower costs and greater efficiencies. Which is good. Higher productivity and lower costs should theoretically translate into a leap in discretionary income or a rise in the purchasing power of every dollar we earn *all else being equal*. Which is double good. Only there is a hitch.

To purchase these lower-priced goods and services and enjoy the promised higher standard of living that productivity has historically delivered, it goes without saying that people must have jobs and sound income. Without them, no matter how efficient, low-cost, and high-quality goods and services become through technological advances, people won't have the means to purchase them. And if people can't purchase them, the long-established relationship between greater productivity and a rising standard of living becomes illusory.

The Double-Edged Sword

Herein lies the double-edged sword of the fourth industrial revolution. Although smart machines and artificial intelligence are predicted to bring unimaginable efficiencies, they will do so by increasingly replacing a wide swath of existing human jobs. While historically jobs have always been around for human beings through technological revolutions, we have never had a technological revolution that has been capable of displacing so many human beings and so much human brain power as the one we are transitioning through now.

According to a report from Oxford Economics, a global forecasting and quantitative analysis firm, smart machines are expected to displace about 20 million manufacturing jobs across the world over the next decade, including more than 1.5 million in the United States.[3] Other studies predict that smart machines, robotics, artificial intelligence, blockchain technology, 3D printing, and automation will put 20 percent to 40 percent of existing jobs at risk over the next decades. And a report from the Brookings Institution finds that 25 percent of US workers will face "high exposure" and risk being displaced over the upcoming few decades. That translates to about 36 million jobs at risk of elimination, with another 52 million— 36 percent—facing "medium exposure" to displacement.[4] The bottom line in all these studies is that we can expect a high level of dislocation and a great release of labor, especially in the transition years as the economy adapts to the new reality.

Poor lower- and middle-class workers, you might think. But high-end jobs are equally at stake as AI and smart machines reach human levels of performance. You don't have to look into the future to see this. Consider the elite sector of Wall Street investing. Already major investment companies are replacing employees with computerized stock-trading algorithms that far outperform them. In the next decade, financial institutions are expected to have replaced 10 percent of their human workforce, with some 35 percent of those jobs in the domain of money management.[5] And consider journalism, where robots have begun writing reports on economic trends, and automation is even now used to generate election and sports coverage and to produce digestible articles from financial reports.

Look at dentistry. In 2017, a robot dentist in China, without human intervention, successfully implanted 3D-printed teeth into a woman's mouth in less than an hour. Only four years earlier, a study at Oxford University had identified dentists and orthodontists as having among the safest jobs vis-à-vis smart robots.[6] And wildlife-preservation researchers responsible for tracking endangered species are on track to becoming endangered themselves. They're increasingly being replaced by drones that capture footage which machine-learning systems then analyze to monitor the populations and movement of endangered species.

Research papers report that AI is in some respects even more accurate than trained radiologists in detecting lung cancer, the most common cause of cancer death in the United States, and in detecting breast cancer, the most prevalent form of cancer in women. In the lung cancer study, published in *Nature Medicine*, the deep learning algorithm performed with 94.4 percent accuracy in spotting cancer that doctors already knew was present. The AI's performance was similar to doctors' when additional tomography scans were available to the radiologists. However, absent these, the AI was more accurate with 11 percent fewer false positives and 5 percent fewer false negatives.[7] In the breast cancer study, which utilized DeepMind (a company owned by Google) and was published in *Nature*, the applied AI proved better at detecting breast cancer than doctors; the AI system was able to reduce false negative mammograms by 5.7 percent in the United States, where readings tend to be done by only one radiologist.[8]

Machine-learning-automated decision-making systems will become responsible for tasks such as writing contracts, approving loans, appraising real estate, deciding whether a customer should be onboarded, and identifying corruption and financial crime—currently all largely human tasks. While human intelligence once directed and controlled machines, this role is increasingly being taken over by smart machines with serious implications for human jobs. Humans must grapple with the challenging reality that AI is even capable of creating art, poems, complex essays, and music, once thought of as domains unique to humans.[9]

Today, owing to technology developments, scores of large companies have fewer employees than they did twenty years ago, even when they've experienced rising sales. Procter & Gamble, for example, increased its sales from $40 billion in 2000 to $67 billion in 2018, yet reduced its workforce in the same period from 110,000 to 92,000. And although sales at General Motors, once the auto king of the world, shrank from $166 billion in 1998 to $147 billion in 2018, a drop of roughly 12 percent, the number of its employees plummeted from 608,000 to 173,000—a loss of 71 percent—during the same period. It certainly seems that the productivity unleashed by technology is reducing the need for labor across industries. And the fourth industrial revolution hasn't even fully hit.

When companies can increasingly make more money with fewer people, many people will feel increasingly irrelevant. But companies can't afford to employ inefficient workers if their aim is to remain competitive. The choice they face is *not between* protecting employees and adopting the new technologies. It *is between* modernizing and becoming irrelevant. And few companies are going to choose irrelevance—nor should we want them to. There's reason.

Pushing or shaming companies to protect workers who are no longer needed is pushing companies to be inefficient and globally noncompetitive, and ultimately to shrink or go out of business, which would result in an even greater loss of jobs and a huge loss of social good.

Essentially, we are entering a new era in which the efficacy of technological advances is hitting a tipping point. These advances will increasingly replace a wide range of human jobs with a new labor force like Alexa, Siri, and Bixby, which doesn't need to check social media, receive a paycheck, take vacations, eat, or even rest.[10]

Where Will the Needed New Jobs Come From?

The imperative question is: Where will all this released human capital find new work? If people cannot find new jobs, we can expect deep social, economic, and psychological ramifications.

Ultimately, of course, the new technologies will create jobs that don't exist today and that we might not even be able to currently imagine. Think about website designers before the internet, or search-engine optimizers, or all the new jobs that sprang up around social media. Perhaps no one could really have predicted that those jobs would appear to support the new technology.

Smart machines such as AI-powered chatbots are on track to fill many human jobs in technical support and customer relations. But we can also imagine that new jobs will arise around programming and developing chatbots' artificial intelligence with the information needed across industries to respond meaningfully to people. Likewise, the development, design, and build-out of new platforms like the metaverse that companies have been buzzing about will create some level of new jobs, as will the mounting energy around bitcoin, decentralization including peer-to-peer networks, and new payment rails. But that takes time. And as Daniel Susskind's book *A World Without Work* highlights, jobs are likely to be under threat from emerging technologies and robotics in a way they never were from earlier technological revolutions.[11]

At the company level, a popular response to the jobs challenge is upskilling and reskilling. Both are important for putting employees in a position to take on these new jobs as they materialize. Amazon, for example, has announced plans to invest $700 million to retrain and upskill 100,000 of its employees to meet the demands of the technology revolution. But the company has also noted that workers may nevertheless still need to find employment opportunities elsewhere. So even though Amazon is going the extra mile to help employees transition into new, technology-related roles, the net number of jobs it will need with the advent of the new technologies is still likely to shrink relative to its sales. To illustrate, beyond greater use of robots in its fulfillment centers, the company has been taking steps to implement federally approved drones to deliver packages to people's homes. Amazon currently employs thousands of outside contractors for last-mile deliveries. Should drone delivery materialize, many of those jobs would become extinct.

Upskilling and reskilling are essentially a supply-side response to the challenge of the fourth industrial revolution. But as the Amazon example reveals, supply-side readiness doesn't guarantee that demand-side jobs will be there to greet released employees.

From Supply-Side Readiness to Demand-Side Jobs

What to do? Where will all the needed jobs come from as companies and the economy transition to the new technological reality?

How can we manage that displacement and buffer the negative effects on people's jobs, and on the economic and social stability of local communities, during the transition phase?

Skills retraining will be part of the answer. So will other efforts that have been proposed, such as financially supporting the displaced, tax breaks for investments in human capital, and buttressing vulnerable local economies and communities. Although these ideas have merit and a role to play, they don't address what we believe is the root of the problem. None of them actually create jobs—what our economies need most, and what gives people's lives purpose. Like upskilling and reskilling, they are all supply-side responses to the challenges caused by artificial intelligence and smart machines.

Jobs matter.

People prosper when they have jobs that allow them to support themselves and their families. Communities and societies that lack jobs often become emotionally and physically unhealthy environments that foster drug use, despondency, and crime as people's free time expands and their lives lose direction and meaning. A lack of gainful employment makes people both unproductive and potentially dangerous to the stability of society at large. If there is a widespread rush toward labor-saving and cost-saving technology, especially AI, without a compensating increase in new jobs, a socially dangerous situation can exist until new jobs are created to offset the losses.

The challenge is how to reduce the negative human impact of the technological revolution without losing its benefits. To do that, we need to match supply-side readiness with demand-side jobs—which brings us right back to the central growth driver that we've been discussing from the very start of this book: market-creating innovation.

95

The success of technology and the productivity it unleashes raise the premium on creativity and the creation of new markets.

While all new markets hold the promise of creating new growth and jobs, helping to close the jobs gap, those based on disruptive creation do so at the cost of existing jobs in the short to medium term. Look no further than the expected impact of autonomous vehicles. Nearly 3 percent of the US workforce, or about 5 million people, support their families by driving taxis, buses, delivery trucks, tractor trailers, and other vehicles. In most US states, truck driver is one of the most common jobs. Although the disruptive creation of autonomous vehicles will surely create new jobs over time, all those current jobs will be in immediate danger as self-driving vehicles start to displace standard cars and trucks.

The challenge for governments and society will be to create new jobs that don't displace others. That is as much an economic imperative as it is a moral one—which is another key reason why nondisruptive market creation is about to become even more important. Microfinance has helped nearly 140 million people with loans to create microenterprises and be gainfully self-employed. Life coaching, another nondisruptive industry, is estimated to have created tens of thousands of new jobs, just as environmental con-sulting has already created thousands of new jobs, and that number is likely only to increase as public concern mounts over environ-mental degradation and climate change. And we can imagine that Space Force will give rise to tens of thousands of new jobs. Nondis-ruptive creation helps ensure that everybody can come on this journey. And the technological advances of the fourth industrial revolution can be leveraged to achieve this.

Nondisruptive creation is not *the* answer to the jobs challenge posed; there are many other pieces to the puzzle that are needed.[12] But it is on track to become an increasingly important way to help

TABLE 4-1

Two key emerging forces and the rising importance of nondisruptive creation

Two key emerging forces	Core implications	Nondisruptive creation
Stakeholder capitalism	The rising movement toward a socially responsible form of capitalism that is less tolerant of social disruption	Is a sustainable approach to innovation as growth can be achieved *without* disruptive consequences to society
The fourth industrial revolution	The rising challenge of job loss as smart machines and AI replace humans	Generates needed new jobs *without* displacing existing ones

address this challenge by creating new jobs with little displacement of existing ones.

Table 4-1 captures the key points of our discussions on these two key emerging trends.

Governments Take Note

The rise of stakeholder capitalism and the fourth industrial revolution have created a need and opened an opportunity for fresh thinking in economic policy about growth and job creation over the next generations.

It is smart and prudent to encourage businesses and entrepreneurs to adopt new technologies. And disruptive creation will remain important to the renewal of industries, especially those that have become dysfunctional owing to inefficient, high-cost, and low-quality production and outputs stemming from obsolete infrastructure or fixed assets. But when it comes to growth and the basic

R&D that governments fund, besides disruptive creation, policy makers would be wise to raise awareness of the importance of nondisruptive creation. An effective economy is not only one that grows and modernizes, but one where no one gets left behind, and we can all participate in it and enjoy its fruits. One way to help society move in this direction is to use our human ingenuity to create new markets and new jobs in a nondisruptive way. Politicians and policy makers in particular should take this message to heart in formulating regional and national innovation strategies so that they can help minimize the social conflicts and costs of innovation and growth while fostering business prosperity.

Hence as both a policy response and a business response, non-disruptive creation is likely to grow in importance. Companies can utilize a measure of the capital liberated by the technology and productivity leaps of the fourth industrial revolution to make invest-ments in nondisruptive creation without redirecting capital away from existing uses.

Growth without job creation is costly and perilous for any soci-ety. Even when growth offers many more job opportunities in the long run, governments need to deal with its social adjustment costs and pain if it comes with disorderly displacement. Along with dis-ruptive creation that evidently has its own distinctive strengths, governments would be wise to create policies in support of the complementary growth path of nondisruptive creation to sustain the healthy progress of both business and society.

Clarity and Action Come with Understanding

We know that huge change is underway. We know that further huge change is right around the corner. But the number of jobs that will be lost and created is not predetermined. That number will ultimately depend on the actions we take (or don't take) and the policies we apply (or don't apply) to meet this challenge. It is up to us to create the future of work and growth that we want. But to do so, we need to understand, among other things, what triggers disruptive growth versus nondisruptive growth, and what a full model of innovation and growth looks like. Then you can assess what kind of growth—disruptive or nondisruptive—your innovation efforts are on track to unleash, and how you can strike a healthy balance between the two. In the next chapter, we directly address these issues and more as we build a growth model for market-creating innovation that pulls together all our learning up to this point.

Chapter Five

The Three Paths to Market-Creating Innovation and Growth

The universal law of cause and effect states that for every cause, there is an effect, and for every effect, there is a cause. Eat too much food and you are likely to gain weight. Here, food is a cause; weight gain is an effect. When we understand cause-and-effect relationships, we are better able to be intentional in our lives. We understand what actions trigger what effects. Then we can determine what outcomes we aim to achieve and how to effectuate them. So if we wish to maintain a healthy weight, we understand that we should not overindulge in food but should eat in moderation.

The law of cause and effect is equally at play and equally valuable when it comes to innovating new markets. But to take advantage of it and become intentional in your innovation efforts, you first need to understand what those relationships are. You need to understand what triggers one type of market-creating innovation over another. And you need to have the full picture—one that embraces both disruptive and nondisruptive creation, since they are complementary and create new growth both separately and together. Focusing on only one will give you an incomplete and biased assessment of market-creating opportunities, limiting your vision of the immense potential for creating the markets of tomorrow.

What leads to one type of market-creating innovation over another? What elicits nondisruptive rather than disruptive creation? And how can you and your team get a complete picture of market-creating innovation in order to have meaningful discussions about it? Although these questions are crucial in assessing an organization's new-market-creation efforts and being strategic in those efforts, current innovation theory lacks a clear unifying framework with which to address them.

We have found that what triggers one type of market-creating innovation over another largely comes down to the type of problem or opportunity you set out to address. In other words, the type of problem or opportunity you set out to tackle is the *cause* prompting the type of market-creating innovation—the *effect*—you are on track to unlock.

The Three Paths to Market-Creating Innovation and Their Growth Consequences

Our research revealed three overarching paths to innovating new markets:

102

FIGURE 5-1

A growth model of market-creating innovation strategy

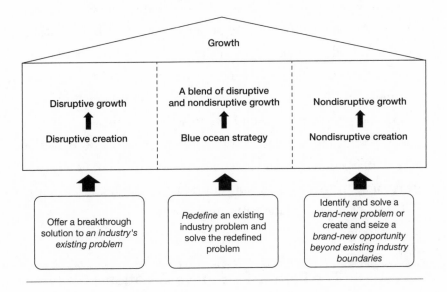

- Offer a breakthrough solution to an industry's existing problem.

- Redefine an industry's existing problem and solve the redefined problem.

- Identify and solve a brand-new problem or create and seize a brand-new opportunity *beyond* existing industry boundaries.

Figure 5-1 provides an overall framework that captures the three paths and shows how each triggers a different balance between disruptive and nondisruptive growth.[1] As seen in the figure, offering a breakthrough solution to an industry's existing problem sets you on the path to disruptive creation and disruptive growth. Identifying and solving a brand-new problem or seizing a brand-new opportunity outside existing industry boundaries sets you on the path to nondisruptive creation and nondisruptive growth. Between these two ends of the market-creating-innovation spectrum is redefining an existing industry problem and then solving the redefined problem. This is the essence of blue ocean strategy, which generates a more balanced blend of disruptive and nondisruptive growth.[2]

Understanding the model matters, because it will help you be far more purposeful in assessing what type of market-creating innovation and growth you are on track to achieve. This will help you move beyond chance and consciously direct your efforts to the type of market innovation you choose to nurture, be it nondisruptive or not, and deliberately put your resources behind it.

Let's look at each of the paths in turn.

The Path to Disruptive Creation

When an organization creates a breakthrough solution for an existing industry problem, it strikes at the core of existing firms and markets. The result is displacement of the old by the new, whether at the outset or over time, as the new market is created *within* the existing boundaries of the industry. Think of the music business. CDs displaced cassette tapes by providing a breakthrough solution to the existing industry problem of how best to store and replay sound recordings. In contrast to their predecessors, they offered "perfect sound forever," skipping effortlessly from one song to another with none of the crackling and gumming up of twisted cassette tapes. Not surprisingly, the CD fast replaced the cassette as the standard music medium. For years, people were thrilled with CDs—until Apple's iPod came around and offered yet another breakthrough solution to the problem of storing and playing music. People rushed to replace their now passé CDs with the iPod and other MP3 players, which gave them easy access to their entire music library. Then smartphones stepped in and had the same effect on MP3 players. Increasingly few of today's youth have even heard of the iPod, because Apple's iPhone and other smartphones have so effectively displaced it. In each case, the existing product and market were essentially replaced by the breakthrough solution.

Although each of these breakthrough solutions was largely launched from the high end, breakthrough solutions launched from the low end proceed in much the same way. Take navigation. Although GPS (Global Positioning System) devices in cars revolutionized navigation from the high end and negated the need to keep a road atlas in the glove compartment, the rise of smartphones, Waze, Google Maps, and other mobile navigation apps offered the next breakthrough solution from the low end. Free, easy to use, and completely portable, they largely displaced the use of GPS devices in cars. Today many more people use these navigation apps than ever used automotive GPS.

In cases like these, the breakthrough solution virtually wipes out the incumbent industry and players. In other cases, while the breakthrough solution may be devastating to the core of the existing industry, the displacement may be incomplete. For example, Uber has rapidly displaced a major portion of the taxicab market, and taxi companies and the industry have seen their market shrink notably, have suffered greatly, and have watched the value of their assets tumble. But they haven't been completely displaced.

And although Amazon offered breakthrough solutions—first to book retail and more recently to general retail—that devastated both those industries and their incumbent players, total displacement has not occurred. Independent bookstores still exist, with some of them even seeing a resurgence, as do retail shops—though admittedly they are increasingly fewer and farther between.

FIGURE 5-2

The path to disruptive creation

Offering a breakthrough solution for the existing industry problem strikes at the core of existing firms, triggering displacement of the old for the new and, with it, disruptive growth

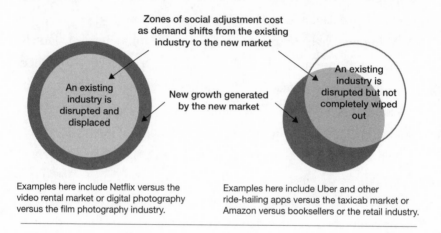

Examples here include Netflix versus the video rental market or digital photography versus the film photography industry.

Examples here include Uber and other ride-hailing apps versus the taxicab market or Amazon versus booksellers or the retail industry.

Figure 5-2 shows the effect of disruptive creation on existing industries and growth. The first set of interlocking circles captures cases of near-to-complete disruption, such as that of CDs by MP3 players, MP3 players by smartphones, the video rental market by Netflix, and the film photography industry by digital photography. The second set of interlocking circles reflects cases in which a breakthrough solution to an existing industry problem disrupts and devastates but does not completely displace an existing industry. Uber and Amazon provide examples.

In either case, as shown in the figure, the breakthrough solution triggers disruptive growth, as existing demand and jobs shift from the incumbent industry to the new market. That's the cost of disruptive creation for society, even though, over time, it attracts new demand by virtue of the breakthrough solution's leap in value. And if the disruptive threat awakens surviving companies and pushes them to up their game for the benefit of consumers, growth is boosted even further. The macro-level outcome of pursuing this innovation path is significant *disruptive growth*.

The Path to Nondisruptive Creation

On the other end of the spectrum, organizations that identify and solve brand-new problems or seize brand-new opportunities *outside* the boundaries of existing industries unlock nondisruptive creation. Instead of looking for breakthrough answers to existing industry problems, this approach begins with asking: Are there brand-new problems we can solve *beyond* existing industry boundaries? Are there brand-new opportunities we can unlock *outside* those boundaries? As your focus shifts in this way, so do the opportunities you see to create new markets that eat at neither the margins nor the core of existing industries and established players. In this way, virtually all the demand created is new, resulting in nondisruptive growth.

While all brand-new problems that are solved in effect result in new opportunities, not all brand-new opportunities are created by addressing new problems. Many of them are generated by spotting and unlocking newly emerging value that is not linked to any unaddressed problem or pain. Consider e-sports: a nondisruptive market offering that addresses an aspiration rather than a problem of youths today. E-sports involves almost no physical activity—just hand-eye coordination, precise timing, skillful planning, and click speed, as an audience watches teams play online video games in massive arenas, their every move projected on panoramic screens. With up to 50,000 in attendance at top e-sport championships and some 100 million watching online in dozens of languages, e-sports has become one of the hottest, most lucrative sports on the planet.

Game makers in the past focused mainly on creating and selling games that were exciting to play—the kind that inspired diehard video-game geeks to lock themselves in their rooms. In the early 2000s, however, they saw a chance to create and seize an opportunity outside the existing industry boundaries. In Korea, where gaming is part of the country's mainstream youth culture, game publishers observed that gamers *and* nongamers excitedly followed online gaming tournaments, commenting on players' tactics and discussing their favorite players and teams in chat rooms.

Game publishers began to realize that there was a huge, untapped market of people who wanted to *watch* others play, whether or not they were gamers themselves—just as people enjoy watching basketball or tennis whether or not they play the game. They also saw the excitement that could potentially be generated by bringing together top gamers from around the world to compete in person for meaningful prize money. The gamers would get the glory of global recognition, the audience would be able to see their favorite players up close, and both would feel the excitement that spectator pro sports have always enjoyed—the thrill of a crowd.

So game publishers started to design games with the aim of creating e-sports, a full-out live spectator sport. That meant creating multiplayer games like Riot Games' *League of Legends* and *Valve* and Hidden Path Entertainment's *Counter-Strike: Global Offensive*, which were as much fun to watch as they were to play, and in which skill and strategy, not luck, were the key to winning. Game makers, along with third-party e-sports organizers, created professional leagues and tournaments around the most skilled players to produce spectacular in-person events and then entered into lucrative agreements for the events to also be broadcast and cast live to fans around the world. In this way, e-sports was crafted into a spectator sport that was separate and distinct from gaming itself.

E-sports took video gaming from kids in a basement to a physical, in-person, pro-sports event. Today, the industry is bigger than ever, with more than $1 billion in revenue and some 175 million e-sports fans around the world. Yet no other pro sport has been disrupted or seen its revenues decline as a result.[3] In fact, more and more pro-sports teams and players see e-sports as a burgeoning growth opportunity for them: members of the New York Yankees in baseball, Magic Johnson and the Houston Rockets in basketball, and the New England Patriots' NFL owner Robert Kraft have bought into the sport.

E-sports created a nondisruptive market by capturing a newly emerging opportunity across the globe. Just like Viagra, GoPro, and men's cosmeceuticals, it was a brand-new offering that lay outside existing industry boundaries when it was created. The same is true for Thinkers50, founded by Des Dearlove and Stuart Crainer. Thinkers50 created a brand-new opportunity for leading management thinkers across the world to meet biannually, become part of a community of peers, and gain insight into the global ranking of ideas, including which ones have the greatest reach and impact and potential to positively shape the future of organizations. The nondisruptive new market unlocked by Thinkers50 neither substitutes for nor displaces an existing industry or existing players in any country or region of the world. Though of a different scale, it, like e-sports, is globally nondisruptive.

But as discussed in chapter 1, nondisruptive market-creating innovation doesn't have to be new to the globe. It can also be and often is regional or country-bound. And it doesn't require inventive or new technology either.

Consider Wecyclers, a trash-to-cash social enterprise that created a nondisruptive new market in Nigeria by identifying and solving a long-unaddressed and taken-for-granted problem that was beyond the boundaries of the existing industry. Nigeria is now Africa's largest economy. In Lagos, its most populous city, only 40 percent of the trash is collected, and almost all of that from wealthy neighborhoods. The rest is thrown in the streets, where it clogs drains and sewers, contributing to stench, filth, flooding, and diseases such as malaria, particularly in the slum neighborhoods where more than 60 percent of the country's 18 million inhabitants live.

The challenge facing the slum communities is twofold: the city requires citizens to pay a fee if they want municipal garbage collection, and few people living in slums can afford it. And even if they could afford it, waste-collecting vehicles can't navigate the narrow, overcrowded roads and alleys in those neighborhoods to reach the dwellers' homes. The founder of Wecyclers, Bilikiss Adebiyi-Abiola, set out not only to solve this problem for the people living in slums, who are financially and logistically out of reach of municipal garbage-pickup service, but also to create a brand-new money-making opportunity for them.

Wecyclers employs a school of drivers who scoot around the slum neighborhoods on low-cost cargo bicycles once a week to collect people's trash. Households may sign up for the free service but must agree to separate their recyclable trash for the pickups. As an incentive, Wecyclers' customers not only get the benefit of no trash and more-sanitary surroundings, but also receive points for every kilogram of trash they recycle. The points may be redeemed at Wecyclers for all kinds of needed and desired goods, from cell phone minutes to basic food items. Wecyclers sells the presorted recyclable items to recycling plants, which use them as low-cost raw materials for other goods. This provides Wecyclers with the funds needed to make its business model work. The result of Wecyclers' nondisruptive creation is a cleaner planet; a cleaner, more-sanitary city; and rising living standards for the poor. While the

FIGURE 5-3

The path to nondisruptive creation

Solving a brand-new problem or creating and seizing a brand-new opportunity outside of existing industry boundaries triggers nondisruptive creation and, with it, nondisruptive growth

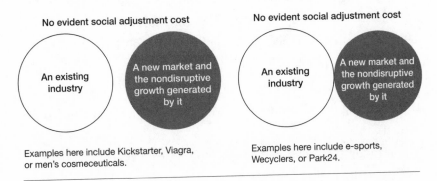

No evident social adjustment cost / No evident social adjustment cost

An existing industry / A new market and the nondisruptive growth generated by it

An existing industry / A new market and the nondisruptive growth generated by it

Examples here include Kickstarter, Viagra, or men's cosmeceuticals.

Examples here include e-sports, Wecyclers, or Park24.

new market created by Wecyclers supplements the existing municipal garbage-collection service, they serve two distinct markets without any overlap.

Figure 5-3 depicts nondisruptive creation as two distinct, non-overlapping circles, with one representing an existing industry and the other a brand-new market created outside existing industry boundaries. The first set of circles captures the creation of a new market—like those for Kickstarter, Viagra, and men's cosmeceuticals—whose boundary is totally distinct from that of an existing industry. The second set captures the creation of a new market whose boundary is tangential to that of an existing industry, as in the cases of e-sports, Wecyclers, and Park24. Either way, solving a brand-new problem or capturing a brand-new opportunity beyond market boundaries strikes at neither the core nor the margins of existing industries. This type of market-creating innovation produces new growth and jobs—and stretches society's imagination. The macro-level outcome of pursuing this path is *nondisruptive growth*.

The Path to Blue Ocean Strategy

Between solving an existing industry problem and identifying and solving a brand-new problem or creating a brand-new opportunity outside industry boundaries lies the path to blue ocean strategy. Here organizations redefine the problem an industry is focused on and solve the redefined problem by looking *across*, not within, industry boundaries in new and creative ways. As figure 5-1 shows, the result is a more balanced blend of nondisruptive and disruptive growth.

Consider Comic Relief, a UK fundraising charity formed in 1985. It redefined the problem the industry focused on, from how to persuade the wealthy to give out of pity and guilt to how to get everybody to do a little something funny for money. It then solved the redefined problem by eliminating factors the charity industry took for granted, such as fancy fundraising galas, year-round solic-itations, marketing, and pity pleas, and created Red Nose Day instead, an event it holds once every two years at which everyone—young, old, rich, or poor—volunteers to perform silly antics to raise money for charity from friends, colleagues, and neighbors. Exam-ples: coming to work in pajamas and hair curlers, a hairy man agreeing to have his back waxed in front of colleagues, or allowing friends to throw a pie in your face, all to raise a little bit of money to help others while having fun.

Unlike conventional fundraising charity organizations, Comic Relief was created *across* existing boundaries of the charity and com-edy industries. It has attracted masses of people. To celebrate Red Nose Day, little red-plastic noses are sold throughout the country for just £1 each, making it easy to take part, have fun, and visually show a commitment to helping positively impact the world. Because

Red Nose Day is held only once every two years, donor fatigue doesn't set in, and people look forward to the next one.

By solving a redefined problem that doesn't go head-to-head with the problem the UK fundraising industry is solving, Comic Relief's market-creating innovation strikes only at the margin, not at the core, of the incumbent industry. The result: although Comic Relief wins a slice of traditional wealthy donors from the fundraising industry, creating a measure of disruptive growth, it also creates new, nondisruptive growth by inspiring an ocean of former nondonors to give. Today, Comic Relief has 96 percent brand awareness in the UK, is almost considered a national holiday, and has raised more than £1 billion in the UK alone.

Similarly, André Rieu and the Johann Strauss Orchestra created a new market by redefining the problem that the classical-music industry focused on. Rieu, dubbed "a maestro for the masses," and his orchestra have consistently appeared on lists of the top-ranking touring concerts worldwide for the past twenty years, along with Coldplay, Beyoncé, and the Rolling Stones. Unlike traditional classical music orchestras, Rieu's combines easy-listening classical and waltz music such as "Blue Danube," "Barcarolle," and "O Mia Babbino Caro" with contemporary music such as Michael Jackson's "Ben" and Celine Dion's hit "My Heart Will Go On," which many people find more accessible. Rieu also moved away from pretentious theaters, choosing instead to hold his concerts in large stadiums with spectacular light and sound effects and a fun, interactive atmosphere much like that at a pop concert. Whereas major concert halls, on average, can seat a maximum of 2,000 people, Rieu's stadiums can easily sell out 10,000-plus seats.

Rieu wins a slice of customers from classical-music concerts and people who once went primarily to pop concerts, but he also creates demand by pulling a mass of new customers, including people who were previously put off by the formality and pretension of classical music or never thought to attend concerts at all. His orchestra strikes at the margins of existing industries, not at their core, by solving a redefined problem that doesn't go head-to-head with the problem that either the classical-music or the pop-music industry is solving.

Or jump to the United States and consider Stitch Fix's multibillion-dollar market-creating innovation. The company redefined the problem on which the online women's-apparel industry was focused, from how to offer choice, low prices, fast delivery, and easy returns to how to curate the perfect look for women so that they could get the expertise of a personal shopper with the lower prices and convenience of online retail. Stitch Fix asks women to answer a list of questions about their body type, size, style, color, and material preferences, occasions for which they are looking to get clothes and accessories (work, date night, casual weekends), and their budget guidelines. The company takes this information, and with the aid of artificial intelligence, a personal shopper pulls together a surprise selection of clothes, shoes, and accessories to create an outfit that matches the shopper's stated need and look, which is sent right to the customer.

Stitch Fix drew a slice of demand from the existing industries of online women's apparel and personal shoppers, creating an element of disruptive growth. But it also created all-new demand in a nondisruptive manner by inspiring and surprising women with fashionable apparel that was just right for them, through affordable and convenient online shopping.

Figure 5-4 captures this approach. As it shows, when organizations redefine problems that industries focus on and then solve the redefined problems, their innovations strike at the margins of existing industries, not at their core. This leads to a modest level of

FIGURE 5-4

The path to blue ocean strategy

Redefining the problem an industry focuses on and solving the redefined problem strikes at the margin(s), not the core, of an existing industry or industries, generating a blend of disruptive and nondisruptive growth

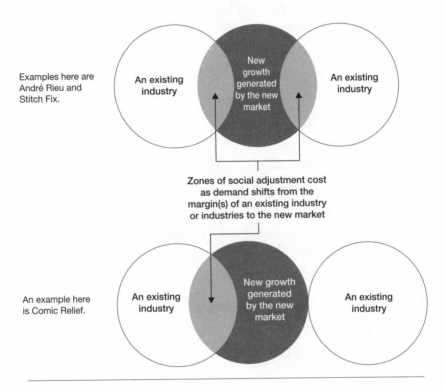

Examples here are André Rieu and Stitch Fix.

An existing industry

New growth generated by the new market

An existing industry

Zones of social adjustment cost as demand shifts from the margin(s) of an existing industry or industries to the new market

An example here is Comic Relief.

An existing industry

New growth generated by the new market

An existing industry

substitution as the new market draws demand at the periphery away from incumbent industries while also creating all-new demand and growth beyond them.

Oftentimes, as with André Rieu and Stitch Fix, a new market draws share from the margins of more than one industry. While Stitch Fix strikes at the peripheries of both the women's online apparel industry and the industry of personal shoppers, André Rieu strikes at the peripheries of both the classical-music and the pop-music industries. The top set of circles in the figure, which shows the new market marginally overlapping with two existing industries, reflects these cases.

The bottom set of circles, by contrast, reflects cases—like that of Comic Relief—in which the redefined problem strikes at the margin of only one existing industry. Although they are created across existing industry boundaries, their disruption is limited to the margin of only one industry. The overlap in both sets of circles shows the area of disruptive growth, while the area beyond the overlap reflects the nondisruptive growth unlocked by the new market.

We've written extensively about the tools and frameworks needed to put blue ocean strategy into action. And a lot has been written about how to disrupt existing industries. What is lacking is guidance on how to effectively realize nondisruptive creation. That is the topic we turn to now and the focus of the second half of our book. Toward this end, the next chapter addresses the right perspectives to lead with for putting nondisruptive creation into practice.

Part Two

How to Realize Nondisruptive Creation

Chapter Six

Lead with the Right Perspectives

For decades, the business and corporate world has been sold on three ideas: One, we should analyze what is, to shape our view of what could be.[1] Two, more than ever today, and even more so in the future, technology innovation is the key to market creation and growth.[2] And three, at the heart of innovation is the lone, smart, and gut-instinct entrepreneur.[3]

Reasonable? Absolutely. Except those are not the right perspectives to lead with to generate nondisruptive creation. Should you consider them? Yes—and act on them too. But you can think of them as the cart, not the horse. And the horse needs to come first.

We have found that people who generate nondisruptive creation lead with certain perspectives and psychological states that differ in many ways from those long-accepted pillars. These perspectives not only open the minds of corporate leaders and make them receptive to nondisruptive opportunities but also are fundamental to the success of their efforts. They exert a powerful influence on their conversations, expectations, and behavior in almost all those leaders do, and help to establish a culture of creativity that is fundamental to nondisruptive creation. The right perspectives illuminate the way before you as we move forward in the next chapters to the concrete building blocks and steps involved in putting nondisruptive creation into practice.

What, then, are the perspectives to lead with? There are three. Let's unpack this.

Flip Your Mental Script

"How can it be?" wondered Mick Ebeling, the founder of the for-profit Not Impossible Labs. In the Nuba Mountains of South Sudan, a young boy named Daniel had lost both his arms. Omar Bashir, then the president of South Sudan, was conducting a campaign of terror, regularly bombing the area with fifty-five-gallon drums filled with jet fuel and shrapnel. The intensity of the explosions left large craters in their wake. The people of the Nuba Mountains knew to flee to the nearest foxhole or cave when planes approached. After they had passed, the people would reemerge and go about their day. Daniel, however, had not been so lucky—nor, as Ebeling was to learn, had thousands of other children and adults.

One day when Daniel was out in the field tending his family's cows, the planes came. There was no foxhole or cave to hide in, so Daniel wrapped his arms around a nearby tree as the bomb exploded. The tree protected his body from the blast, but the force of the bomb blew off his arms. It was already hard enough to stay alive in the region under the harsh conditions and constant bombings. Without arms, it was near to impossible. Daniel said that he would die if he could, because of the overwhelming burden he would now be to his family.

As Ebeling sat in his kitchen in Los Angeles and read this story in *Time*, his young sons were asleep down the hall. He tried to imagine one of them wishing to be dead to spare his parents the burden he imposed on them. So Ebeling decided to do something about the tragic situation. He was told he would never be able to enter the Nuba Mountain region, which was heavily armed. He was reminded that even people in wealthy countries often could not easily afford $15,000 prosthetic limbs. Besides, the limbs could not be fitted to match Daniel's arm stumps. Furthermore, what Daniel needed was not arms to conceal his physical loss but arms and hands that actually worked so that he could become self-reliant again. All true. But Ebeling didn't let what is shape his view of what should be.

Within six weeks Ebeling was on a plane to South Africa with his crew. In his determination, he had learned about a carpenter in South Africa, Richard Van As, who had used a 3D printer to create a mechanical hand after he lost four fingers in a circular saw. The plastic-filament materials were dirt cheap, and with a laptop and a 3D printer, you could build what you needed on the spot. If Ebeling could learn from Van As how he had designed, created, and tested his "robohand," he reasoned, he could translate that learning into cheap, practical arms and hands tailored to fit Daniel. And while doing so, he could teach the local people to become self-reliant in building limbs for other amputees in the Nuba Mountains—creating, in effect, a new offering where none had existed before.

For one week, Ebeling worked every day and night under Van As's tutelage to learn everything he could about Van As's 3D hand and the mechanics behind it that allowed for basic movement. He reached out via email and Skype to Tom Catena, a physician in the Nuba Mountains who had been featured in the *Time* article, for support in finding a simple structure with basic power where Ebeling and his team could work. This turned out to be a local church that supported Catena's work.

Four months from the day Ebeling learned about Daniel's plight, by the grace of Not Impossible Labs and support from Intel, Daniel had simple, working 3D arms and hands that cost all of $150 to make. For the first time in two years, he could hold a spoon and feed himself. But that was just the beginning. By the time Ebeling and his team were back in Los Angeles, he had received a text saying that the local South Sudanese had already built three more arms for amputees. Through the generosity of Intel, they had been left with all the necessary equipment and hundreds of pounds of filament and other materials to continue. The prosthetic 3D printing facility that Not Impossible Labs set up in South Sudan with Intel's support is the first of its kind in the world.

Ebeling's nondisruptive creation has many idiosyncratic features. But those peculiarities aside, the perspective Ebeling led with is no different from the one that Jack Dorsey led with in creating the $70 billion corporation Square, now renamed Block—or, for that matter, the one that any of the firms in our research led with to unlock nondisruptive creation. Dorsey had seen how his former boss (and eventual cofounder), Jim McKelvey, had lost a sale of handblown glass because of a limited capability to accept credit cards. Because handblown glass tends to be an impulse purchase, McKelvey knew that the sale was lost for good. He was not alone. As Dorsey and McKelvey looked into it, they discovered that other individuals and microbusinesses were completely cut off from credit card payment systems, which were dominated by entrenched players with deep pockets who catered to large retailers. The systems are costly, sophisticated, and physically cumbersome, creating nearly insurmountable barriers for individuals and microbusinesses to set themselves up to accept credit card payments. But Dorsey and McKelvey, like Ebeling, did not let current conditions shape their view of what should be. And what should be is that no individual or small business should ever again have to lose a sale through an inability to accept credit card payments. The result, as we know, is a new nondisruptive market.

A challenge at the core of the field of sociology, and of nondisruptive creation, is understanding the relationship between two constructs—what sociologists call *structure* and *agency*. Structure refers to the environment and the world that we experience, which defines our reality. Agency is the power people have to think for themselves and act in ways that create the environment and the world we experience. All firms consider and act on both structure and agency. However, the relationship of the two constructs and their impact on us is profoundly different, depending on which one of the two we lead with.

For decades, the business and corporate worlds have been urged to analyze what is in order to shape their view of what could be. In sociological terms, this view directs us to lead with structure and the environment. It effectively says, "This is the chessboard, and these are the pieces. In light of this, how are you going to play best?" Here the micro actor, the firm, essentially sees itself as a piece on the chessboard, whose rules and dynamics have been largely set by outside forces. That becomes the market reality, the frame—or in academic terms, the bounded rationality by which the firm and its leaders glean their options and take action. In this view, the market and the environment set the stage for what the firm judges to be possible, profitable, and wise, just as in chess, where the "external environment"—the rules and other players' moves—importantly *determines and limits* what move you should make next.

That we have the freedom to create a new game, to consciously untether our thoughts from what is and imagine brand-new possibilities beyond the chessboard, is largely written off from our imagination space. We are conditioned to believe that's not the way the game is played. So we don't play that way. Our agency here is constrained by structure.

In contrast, firms that generate nondisruptive creation lead with agency, as Ebeling, Dorsey, and McKelvey did. Rather than start with the chessboard, they start with their minds and imagination, the magic between their ears, to envision what could be and what should be, irrespective of what is. They flip the script so that their minds, thoughts, and ideas are magnetized to create new realities. In other words, they honor and pay homage first and foremost to the sovereignty of their minds, their imagination, and their free will—to their ability to see otherwise. They recognize their own capacity to change the environment and create the world they envision with different actions.[4]

For this reason, they are not locked in by the bounded rationality of the world as it is. They openly question and reimagine all the things that those who lead with structure accept as givens, asking, *Why not? What if?* That allows them to see what others can't see. To question what others don't question. And to reinterpret what is possible and how to achieve it. And yet, most of us unknowingly give this power away. When we use our imaginations, we tend to use them the wrong way—to imagine why something won't work or can't be done, not why and how it can be achieved.

Think of Ebeling reading that *Time* article. If you lead with structure, you're likely to sigh, shake your head in dismay at the trying conditions, and believe that there's not much you can do. You'll most likely be too overwhelmed by what is to even use your imagination, as Ebeling did to create a brand-new opportunity, and then creatively seek out ways to make that happen, as Not Impossible Labs did by partnering with Intel and tracking down Richard Van As. Same with Dorsey and McKelvey. Lead with structure, and the small and infrequent transactions of individuals and microbusinesses would hardly inspire the creation of a new nondisruptive market. Instead, our imagination would most likely jump in to convince us why the current situation is what it is and to move on.

A fair question, then, is why has leading with agency taken a backseat to structure, when leading with agency is what creates brand-new opportunities and solves brand-new problems to make our world better? One reason is that academics can't easily measure it, so studies are fewer. Academic research gravitates toward what can be measured—which is what's seen, not what isn't seen. So the environment has long been the starting point, even though that means diverting leaders from their greatest strength and truest source of wealth: their imaginations and their free will to rise above the world as we know it and create the future. Because of this, leading with agency becomes a harder sell. It seems much more reasonable to argue that we should begin with what is. But reasonable doesn't create nondisruptive markets.

Improving the current market reality through incremental innovation or a breakthrough solution that disrupts and re-creates the existing chessboard is a big deal. And it brings many benefits to our economies. But a focus on what is can obscure the realization that—using your imagination and agency—you can create a new chessboard without disrupting what is.

Leading with the right mental script is the first requisite for generating nondisruptive creation. The next is holding the right perspective on how to think about and deal with technology.

Don't Confuse the Means with the Ends

Nowadays, it is easy to be seduced by technology. Many companies and startup founders see technology innovation as the path to market creation. They focus on how to engineer and shoehorn the latest technologies into new market offerings they hope will take off. Then they get burned when the market they're aiming to create doesn't materialize because people—plain and simple—are not convinced of the value it will deliver to them.

This brings us to the second perspective nondisruptive creators lead with: they don't confuse the means with the ends. They see technology as a great enabler but realize that *value innovation*— offering buyers a leap in value—is what ultimately creates a nondisruptive new market. This may sound counterintuitive, because technology is a critical element of so many market innovations, whether nondisruptive or disruptive. But don't be fooled.

Although new technologies are often major factors in nondisruptive creation, what determines whether a nondisruptive new market takes off and is commercially viable is when these new technologies are driven first and foremost by a step change in value for buyers. Too many firms get the sequence wrong. They think, "If we pursue technology innovation, then we'll be successful." We are saying that you must reverse this. If you pursue value innovation, you will be on the path to opening a compelling nondisruptive new market. Value innovation is what inspires demand behavior, which is real value in use. That applies to blue ocean strategy and disruptive creation as well.[5]

Value innovation can be attained using new technology, as in the nondisruptive cases of Square (now named Block), Viagra,

M-PESA, and e-sports. But it can also be attained by combining existing off-the-shelf technology, as Music: Not Impossible did, or even with little or no technology, as in the cases of Wecyclers, life coaching, and Halloween pet costumes. What is nonnegotiable, however, is that it makes a positive difference in the way we live and work. Nondisruptive creators think value innovation first, and then technology. What is the compelling leap in value you deliver?

Why, then, do many economists appear to argue otherwise?

Economic studies on growth and innovation often seem to prove this second perspective wrong—to, in effect, show that technology innovation is what matters most.[6] There's good reason for this stance, which is worth taking a moment to explore, because we often got pushback on this point in the course of our research. Economic studies on growth and innovation have long focused on the impact of technology innovation. Despite obvious differences among them, they have generally found that technology innovation is positively related to growth—higher technology innovation generates higher growth. But there is an important difference between these studies and our research: the level of analysis. A close look reveals that they are looking at the macro level (countries, regions, societies, or even industries) or the meso level (interactions or game dynamics of market players). In contrast, our analysis is at the micro level of the individual firm and its profitable growth. And what you find is that what holds true at the macro or the meso level does not necessarily hold true at the level of the individual firm.

That's because whether a particular firm makes money on its technology innovation is largely irrelevant, especially at the macro level of economic analysis. What *is* relevant there is whether the basket of technological possibilities from which all firms can draw to spur macroeconomic growth has enlarged. A relevant question there is: Can the creation of the technology breakthrough of AI, for example, be leveraged and deployed by innumerable firms in diverse industries to create new growth at the macro level? So whether or not the technology creator commercializes and captures the economic rent of its technology is not of prime concern, because if not the creator, then some other firms will achieve success by linking the innovation to value, thereby increasing the macro growth rate of the economy by effectively leveraging this technology breakthrough.

Take the classic example of Xerox PARC. It was shuttered even though it created countless technological innovations, such as the graphical user interface (GUI) on all phones and computers today. The company didn't achieve commercial success or directly create new markets or growth with GUI and many of its other technological innovations. But it did increase the bundle of technologies from which other firms could draw to innovate new markets. Steve Jobs and Apple were among the first to do just that. When Jobs visited Xerox PARC, he was impressed by the potential of GUI. So he skillfully took Xerox PARC's technological innovation of GUI and linked it to value by creating a simple, intuitive interface that ordinary people could understand and feel comfortable using. This allowed Apple to usher in the new market of personal computers and later to create the iOS that powers many of its mobile devices, such as iPod Touch and the iPhone. Eventually other firms followed suit.

The macro economy grew as a result of Xerox PARC's technological innovation, confirming the conclusions of many economists. But Xerox PARC itself failed commercially. It was Apple's value innovation that triggered the growth made possible by Xerox PARC's GUI. So although technology innovation is indeed a key contributor to economic growth at the macro level, the same cannot necessarily be said at the individual-firm level. In fact, industrial organization studies—a chapter of microeconomics—that have examined the effects of technology innovation on individual-firm performance have been inconsistent, ranging from positive to neutral to negative depending on how the variables were measured.[7]

The lesson is, be clear what your intent is and stay focused on how to achieve it. If you want to ensure the commercial success of your nondisruptive creation and reap the rewards of your time and investment, you need to keep your eyes on the prize, and that prize is value innovation. Successful nondisruptive creators think value innovation first, and then technology to achieve that end. If you get the sequence wrong, you are likely to find your nondisruptive creation slow to take off or, worse, dead on arrival.

Unlock the Many, Not Only the Few

Do you ever use Liquid Paper—the opaque white liquid that you dab on to cover writing or typing mistakes? You know the stuff. You're filling in some form and all of a sudden you realize you entered the wrong info on the wrong line, so you have to white it out before you can correct it. Created in the 1950s, Liquid Paper, originally called Mistake Out, opened up a huge, nondisruptive new market. At the time, secretaries across the United States were struggling to remove mistakes made on typewriters. To correct an error, they essentially had to retype the page, creating obvious stress, additional work, and a lot of costly lost time. Liquid Paper changed that and rapidly became an indispensable tool for secretaries, for kids at school, and for many of the rest of us.

Today Liquid Paper is owned by Newell Brands. But this nondisruptive innovation was created not by an entrepreneur, an innovation expert, or a scientist but by Bette Nesmith Graham, a single mother who worked as a secretary at a Texas bank. To earn a bit of extra money to support herself and her young son, Michael (who grew up to become a member of the pop rock group the Monkees), Graham would use her hobby—painting—to decorate windows in the bank during holiday season. She realized that a painting error is never erased—it's painted over. So she started to use white tempera paint, which she brought to the office in a bottle, to paint over her typing mistakes. Although some of her bosses rebuked her for using the paint, her colleagues wanted her "mistake out."

Ever since Joseph Schumpeter, the father of innovation, put the entrepreneur on a pedestal, the cult worship of entrepreneurs has been off and running. In Schumpeter's world, their creativity, daring, and gut instincts are the central drivers of growth, innovation, and the creation of new markets. According to Schumpeter, the entrepreneur is a scarce resource to be cherished.

But as the myth of the entrepreneur has become deeply entrenched in our psyches and minds, a cognitive barrier has arisen that tends to separate the lone and instinctive entrepreneur, or "creative," from everyone else. Such separation may be an unintended consequence of Schumpeter's thought, but it narrows our view of the sources of ingenuity and innovation.

Which brings us to the third perspective nondisruptive creators lead with.

They cherish entrepreneurs or "creative" people but recognize that overemphasizing them leads to underemphasizing the creativity and contributions of everyone else. As a result, a vast expanse of human creativity and ideas risk going overlooked and unappreciated, even though that's precisely what's needed to solve brand-new problems outside industry boundaries and create and seize brand-new opportunities to realize nondisruptive creation. While it took more than the initial idea of Graham, a secretary and frustrated user of typewriters, whose ingenuity wasn't appreciated at her work, to realize the multimillion-dollar nondisruptive Liquid Paper market, a company should not overlook ideas like this by taking a narrow view of the sources of creativity.

It's well established that children are creative. Think of the make-believe games they conjure up, the creative reasons they give for eating dessert before vegetables, or the wild-eyed stories they imagine and tell. But creativity isn't just the province of youth. It's the province of young, old, educated, and uneducated. For proof look no further than social media, where we learn every day that creativity, humor, style, and initiative are hardly the province of a few but are had by the many. Mohammad Yunus, the creator of microfinance, saw ingenuity and resilience in the extremely poor, and they proved him right. In a study published in *Management Science*, a leading academic journal, a group of innovation academics and 3M managers found that insights garnered from general frontier practitioners like Graham were important in addressing problems or opportunities that are new to the world.[8]

Of course, not all people are equally creative. But most are creative enough. In fact, since Aristotle, the idea of *the wisdom of crowds*, which taps into this awareness of people's inborn ingenuity and the power of drawing on a diversity of perspectives, has been discussed. Popularized by James Surowiecki in his book of the same name, it explores how a group of seemingly regular people can be collectively better at solving problems and fostering innovation than even the brightest individual.[9] Although the topic has been studied under other names, such as "crowd science," "collective wisdom," and "creative intelligence," the basic thrust of the idea has been consistent: given certain positive dynamics in a group, such as the diversity of its members, collective wisdom can be superior to that of an elite few.[10]

In fact, the history of business and economics has been and will continue to be written by both gifted entrepreneurial leaders and the wisdom of crowds. To realize market-creating innovation, particularly nondisruptive creation, we need to take a broad view of creativity and innovativeness, embracing the fact that they are ubiquitous and that everybody can contribute to them alongside gifted entrepreneurs, thus maximizing the chances for commercial success.

It takes a network of people with differing perspectives and skills to bring any nondisruptive creation into existence—to cultivate, refine, and collectively figure out what must be learned or unlearned and where the clues are as you draw from here and there and put it all together to realize your new offering. As nature teaches us, no fruit is born without cross-pollination. Or as Mick Ebeling put it, "When you are creating what's never been created before, you aren't sure what it will take. You need all minds on deck, so we have everyone's brains and voices in the game. We draw on people near and far, just as Not Impossible Labs tapped into the insight of South African carpenter Richard Van As, Intel, physiotherapists, and engineers in the case of Daniel, or the profoundly deaf pop singer and songwriter Mandy Harvey (an *America's Got Talent* 'Golden Buzzer' winner) in creating Music: Not Impossible." He adds, "We hold nothing back and actively share even the seemingly most naive and counterintuitive ideas. But often therein lies the genius. Everyone's got something to contribute."[11]

Table 6-1 depicts the three perspectives needed to generate nondisruptive creation. They will ensure that you are looking in the right direction and will guide your conversations, reasoning, and

TABLE 6-1

Moving toward the perspectives needed for generating nondisruptive creation

Conventional perspectives	Nondisruptive perspectives
See the existing market and environment as teeing off and setting the stage for what is possible and profitable; *agency is constrained by structure*	*Lead with agency over structure* and refuse to be bound by the world as it is; individual firms can imagine and create brand-new opportunities beyond the existing market and environment
See technology innovation as the *path* to market creation; here, *new technologies* become the focus	Think *value innovation* first, then seek *enablers like technology* to realize the intended value innovation
Entrepreneurs and *creative people* are the *central drivers* of market-creating innovation	*Gifted individuals as well as the wisdom of crowds* are important in creating new markets

judgment. By sharing the right perspectives and discussing how and why they matter, your team can collectively build a culture of creativity needed to generate nondisruptive creation. Probe: Are we leading with structure or with our agency? Do we think technology first, or value innovation and offering a magnitude of real value in use? And are we looking only to the few for ideas and answers, or are we tapping into the creativity of the many?

These questions and three perspectives can provide a compass for your thinking and efforts in the process of creating a nondisruptive market. With this compass in mind, we are now ready to move to the next chapter, where we will lay out the three building blocks needed to create a nondisruptive market. We then zoom in on the first one, where we outline the concrete actions and tools to identify, frame, and assess nondisruptive opportunities in a meaningful and motivating way.

Chapter Seven

Identify a Nondisruptive Opportunity

H aving clarified what perspectives you should lead with to open your mind and increase the creative voices you draw on to unlock a commercially compelling nondisruptive opportunity, the next step is moving from thought to action. C-level executives who are thinking about pushing for growth and innovation, practitioners who are asked to bring that intent to life, and entrepreneurs who are considering launching new businesses need to understand the practical steps and tools to turn aspiration into reality.

To meet this challenge, we studied whether a pattern exists in the creation process and if so, what it looks like so that we could decipher the process of "how." Our aim was to pinpoint the recurring thought processes and actions of nondisruptive creators and codify them. Then other organizations could apply the pattern to more successfully put nondisruptive creation into practice.

FIGURE 7-1

The three building blocks for realizing nondisruptive creation

The third building block: Realize the opportunity
Secure the enablers needed to realize the opportunity in a high-value, low-cost way

The second building block: Find a way to unlock the opportunity
Challenge the existing assumptions that have concealed the opportunity and reframe them to discover a way to unlock it

The first building block: Identify a nondisruptive opportunity
Identify a brand-new problem or opportunity that you would like to pursue

At the highest level, our research revealed three basic building blocks common to organizations and individuals who have created and captured a nondisruptive new market. As seen in the figure 7-1, the first building block involves identifying a nondisruptive opportunity to pursue. The second involves unearthing and articulating the existing assumptions that have concealed the opportunity and reframing them to find a way to unlock it. And the third involves securing the enablers needed to realize the opportunity in a high-value, low-cost way. The building blocks can be broadly regarded as action steps.

In this chapter, we'll examine the specifics of the first building block and its corresponding tools and frameworks. In the subsequent two chapters, we'll do the same with building blocks two and three.

The First Building Block: Identify a Nondisruptive Opportunity

How can organizations identify a nondisruptive opportunity that exists outside industry boundaries? To begin, be clear that your objective is not to disrupt or compete but to solve a brand-new problem or create and seize a brand-new opportunity. A clear intention will keep your mind focused on nondisruptive creation so that you don't unconsciously defer to the familiar concepts of compete and disrupt in your market-creating efforts. You want to think about pressing but overlooked issues in the world, in your industry, in your vocation, or in our lives that you are passionate about and that people or organizations are struggling with—or about burning but unseized opportunities that could, if created, make a real difference in the lives of people and communities.

When we care deeply about something, it usually means that the issue is of central importance. If people or organizations are struggling with it, and if solving it could make a real difference, the issue is most likely linked to a promising nondisruptive opportunity for which there is a real market.

Passion also matters because it sustains our will and drive to persist despite the inevitable stumbles and constraints we all face on a journey of creation. You won't be so easily tempted to throw in the proverbial towel. As people, we naturally crave problems to solve and yearn to make a positive difference to others. We also derive immense intrinsic gratification from creating meaningful opportunities for others. These internal motivations will inspire you and your team on your journey. They are enormous sources of energy.

As we discussed in chapter 1, Arunachalam Muruganantham, who created the simple sanitary pad–making machine sold directly to rural Indian women, was deeply passionate about rural women's health where over 200 million Indian women relied on dirty rags, ash, or were banished to huts during their monthly cycle due to not being able to stay clean. Muruganantham's passion ran so deep he was not deterred even as his village deemed him possessed and planned a type of exorcism that involved hanging him upside-down in a tree. While Muruganantham was forced to flee his village, his passion for women's health and well-being led him to never quit. Perry Chen, Yancey Strickler, and Charles Adler, the founders of Kickstarter, were passionate about the importance of creativity and artists' deepest aspirations to realize their artistic dreams. Cameron Stevens and his cofounders of Prodigy Finance were passionate about advanced studies abroad, seeing global education as a pathway to change young people's lives and create a broader understanding of the world.

Two Avenues to Nondisruptive Creation

We found that companies and individuals can take two primary avenues to create a nondisruptive market. As depicted in figure 7-2, one is to address an existing but unexplored issue or problem, and the other is to address a newly emerging issue or problem outside the boundaries of existing industries. Whether you represent a big organization or a small one, and whether your intent is to create a large nondisruptive market or a modest one, the same two avenues apply.

Address an existing but unexplored issue or problem

A brand-new problem or opportunity doesn't necessarily mean that it suddenly popped up and never existed before. Counterintuitively,

FIGURE 7-2

The two avenues to nondisruptive creation

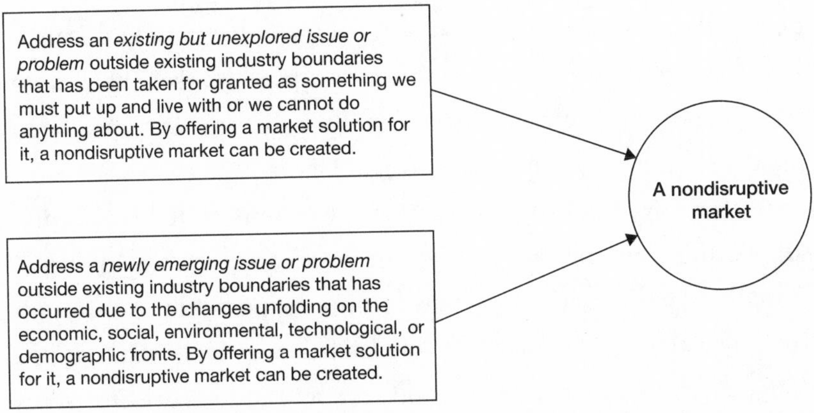

Address an *existing but unexplored issue or problem* outside existing industry boundaries that has been taken for granted as something we must put up and live with or we cannot do anything about. By offering a market solution for it, a nondisruptive market can be created.

Address a *newly emerging issue or problem* outside existing industry boundaries that has occurred due to the changes unfolding on the economic, social, environmental, technological, or demographic fronts. By offering a market solution for it, a nondisruptive market can be created.

A nondisruptive market

a brand-new problem or opportunity may be one that has long existed but—importantly—has remained unexplored because it hasn't been seen as a problem to solve or an opportunity to create through a market. Sometimes that's because the issue has been viewed as merely a fact of life that people have consciously or unconsciously accepted as simply "the way things are." Sometimes it's because long ago a reputable organization or individuals may have tried to address the issue and failed, so people have regarded it as essentially impossible or untouchable, squelching efforts to make another attempt.

An existing problem or opportunity may also be taken for granted and accepted because people have patched together some form of nonmarket solution to address the issue. For example, people needing postpartum care have long turned to nonmarket solutions such as asking family members or friends to lend a helping hand and provide social support in the months following a birth, which are physically and emotionally taxing for most mothers.

Having spotted a new business opportunity to be created and captured by addressing this issue through a market, postpartum care centers—dedicated residential facilities where new mothers can stay during their physical and mental recovery following childbirth—have been set up, creating a new nondisruptive market. They were started and grown initially by several Korean firms but have been rapidly evolving and mushrooming in Asia.

In this way, nondisruptive markets are often created by turning an existing issue that has been taken for granted as a way of life or something to live with into a new business opportunity. Many nondisruptive market creators have pursued this avenue. Both Grameen Bank and Kickstarter identified and set out to address existing issues that lacked market solutions. In Bangladesh, most of the population had lived for decades on a few dollars a day and were universally deemed not creditworthy. The unintended effect was generational poverty, which was seen and treated as an unfortunate part of life's hard reality—until Mohammad Yunus set out to address this existing but unexplored problem with a market solution.

Kickstarter's founders realized that most creative projects remained inside people's heads, unrealized, for a lack of funding. Kickstarter set out to address this long-standing, ruefully accepted issue with a market solution that would open a brand-new funding opportunity for the artistic community to flourish.

Or take Mick Ebeling and Not Impossible Labs. The fact that profoundly deaf people can't experience music didn't just pop up. It had always existed. But they saw this not as the unfortunate fate and inevitable destiny of the deaf but as a brand-new opportunity to create. So Ebeling, Daniel Belquer, and the rest of the team at Not Impossible Labs set out to change that and offer a market solution to this unaddressed issue with Music: Not Impossible.

Park24 Times, postpartum care centers, the Square Reader, Liquid Paper, Viagra, Wecyclers, Prodigy Finance, and going back in time, the humble but indispensable windshield wiper, dishwasher, and sanitary napkins for women are just a few examples of the countless nondisruptive creations generated by addressing existing but unexplored issues and problems beyond established industry boundaries with market solutions.

Address a newly emerging issue or problem

Addressing an emerging need or issue beyond existing industry boundaries is perhaps the more intuitively evident avenue to nondisruptive creation. Socioeconomic, environmental, demographic, or technological changes that have an impact on society or people's lives give rise to new problems, opportunities, and issues. Offering an effective market solution to an emerging need or issue opens the door to a nondisruptive new market.

Consider the Tongwei Group. With global pressure mounting for clean, low-carbon energy, there was a new push in China for green sources of energy to help meet the country's commitment to cap carbon emissions by 2030. Nowhere was this emerging challenge more pressing than in the provinces in eastern and central China where industrial activities were concentrated and power demand was rising, creating a widening gap between the need for green energy and the existing coal-dominated energy supply. But these regions were densely populated, with most of their rural land reserved for agricultural use, leaving scant usable land on which to build green-energy production facilities.

Seeing this emerging need, the Tongwei Group set out to create a brand-new nondisruptive market of green energy by leveraging its fish-farm business. The Tongwei Group is an aquatic feed provider servicing hundreds of thousands of fish farmers and millions of acres of fish-farm waters in eastern and central China. Although aquaculture was already an important source of revenue for individual farmers and local governments, Tongwei determined that the economic value of these water resources could be multiplied by leveraging the unutilized water surface to produce green energy.

So Tongwei created the nondisruptive, fishery-integrated, photovoltaic (PV) industry, which essentially integrated a water-based PV system with its innovative cage-type aquacultural facilities. Solar panels were set above the water, lowering water temperatures and reducing photosynthesis and algae growth, which boosted the fish farms' output. Meanwhile, above the water, Tongwei generated electricity with its solar farms. The effect of this nondisruptive creation was a higher income for fish farms, a new source of green energy for the regions, more tax revenues for local governments, and a highly profitable new business for Tongwei. By utilizing the water resources of its fish-farming business, Tongwei pioneered and created a unique new market that offers green-energy fish farming that is nondisruptive to anyone and is expanding rapidly across China.

Or forget green energy and let's talk food, namely kimchi. The Korean company Winia Mando identified a $1.5 billion nondisruptive opportunity by addressing a newly emerging issue that Koreans faced. Kimchi, a mixture of fermented cabbage, spices, and garlic, is a staple of the Korean diet. In 2017, Koreans ate an average of three kilograms (about six and a half pounds) of kimchi every month. For a family of four that's more than twenty-five pounds a month. Traditionally Korean families made kimchi in large batches at home, fermented it in clay pots buried in the earth, and kept it there throughout the year to guard the perfect taste and freshness.

In the late 1980s and early 1990s, rapid and massive industrialization and urbanization hit, with Koreans migrating to cities, living in apartments, and leading increasingly hectic lives. Now they lacked a garden in which to bury their clay pots of kimchi. And even those who had a garden no longer wanted to engage in the laborious task of burying clay pots. So they started fermenting and storing kimchi in their refrigerators. But those appliances were significantly inferior to the traditional method of preserving kimchi. It didn't taste nearly as good, it went sour in a week, its pungent odor permeated the other food in the refrigerator, and it took up a lot of space because Koreans ate so much of it.

Winia Mando saw this newly emerging challenge as an opportunity to create a brand-new nondisruptive market. After all, although Koreans' lifestyles had changed, their love for kimchi had not. The result was a nondisruptive market solution called Dimchae, an innovative kitchen appliance designed to mimic the way kimchi was traditionally fermented and stored. Dimchae uses direct cooling (versus the indirect cooling in a traditional refrigerator) and keeps the humidity at a level like that in porous clay pots and the temperature several degrees lower than a traditional refrigerator's. Its cooling is constant and consistent, like that achieved with the clay pots, because the door isn't continually opened and closed, leading to fluctuations in temperature that alter the taste and freshness of kimchi.

Launched in 1996, the new nondisruptive market solution soon became as indispensable to Korean homes as the standard refrigerator continued to be. By 2014, more than 85 percent of Korean households had purchased Dimchae; today that share is more than 90 percent, with a 20 percent growth rate as Koreans retire older models and purchase new ones.

Likewise, the nondisruptive industry of cybersecurity, now valued at more than $160 billion, was created as a direct response to the burgeoning threat of cyberattacks on organizations, triggered by the rapidly emerging confluence of widespread internet access, smartphones, cloud computing, and the internet of things. E-sports, smartphone accessories, men's cosmeceuticals, and pet Halloween costumes are just a handful of the vast array of multimillion- and multibillion-dollar nondisruptive new markets created by addressing newly emerging needs and issues that have an impact on people's lives.

Three Ways of Identifying a Nondisruptive Opportunity

The two avenues can help you understand what problems or opportunities will generate a nondisruptive market and can lead your search efforts in the right direction. Without them, you run a risk of focusing on disruptive problems that won't generate a nondisruptive new market even when they're addressed.

Although knowing *what* is a critical first step, you also need to know *how* to spot these opportunities and bring them into sharp focus, whether they are existing but unexplored or newly emerging. Our research reveals three ways that companies and individuals can follow to identify a nondisruptive opportunity (see figure 7-3).

FIGURE 7-3

The three ways of identifying a nondisruptive opportunity

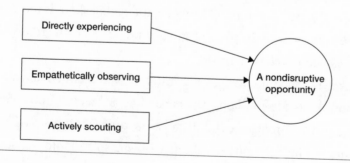

Directly experiencing

When Perry Chen, the eventual cofounder of Kickstarter, had the idea of hosting a concert that would showcase nonmainstream music, he found himself stopped dead in his tracks. Despite his enthusiasm for the idea and his belief that his friends and others would enjoy such a concert, he realized that he wouldn't be able to pull it off for lack of money. And so the concert didn't happen. This deeply bothered Chen. As an artist working in electronic music at the time, he knew that countless other creatives hit a similar wall every day: their art was cut short simply because they couldn't fund it. Chen was certain that a solution to this existing but unexplored problem would really help a lot of artists and was just waiting to happen. That solution was Kickstarter.

Chen is not alone. When Cameron Stevens, who cofounded Prodigy Finance, was working in Malaysia, he decided to apply to INSEAD to get his MBA. INSEAD, a top business school in the world, has a campus in Fontainebleau, France, with 70 percent of its students coming from outside Europe. When the acceptance letter arrived, he was thrilled. But his excitement was soon replaced by frustration and deep disappointment. Lacking local cosigners, collateral, or a credit history in France, he couldn't get a loan. HSBC, the one bank that was willing to discuss financing options with him, asked him to put up 100 percent of liquid assets for a loan of 75 percent of the funds he needed. Stevens recalls, "I said to them: 'I'm not sure you understand how this works. If I had the money in the first place, I wouldn't have asked you for it.' That was just absolutely ridiculous."

Stevens ended up having to defer his enrollment while he worked to save the money for his tuition. After he eventually arrived on campus, he found that the problem he had encountered was a pervasive one. As Stevens reflected, "I saw many people drop out or not arrive on campus due to a difficulty in getting cross-border funding. It was a topic of general conversation among many of my classmates in saying how lots of people didn't come, how hard it was to get funding without 'local' cosigners or collateral. It was a big problem that no one was addressing."[1] So Stevens and his cofounders—Miha Zerko and Ryan Steele—also INSEAD MBA students, set out to solve this taken-for-granted problem with a market solution.

And recall Art Fry, who regularly faced the problem of bookmarks that fell out of his hymnbook at choir practice. He found himself looking over his neighbors' shoulders to see what page the choir was on. He remembered a discovery made by his fellow 3M scientist, Spencer Sheldon, that was sitting unused in 3M's labs: the adhesive that sticks to surfaces but doesn't bond tightly. This got Fry thinking. Could this solve the problem he experienced time and again? More than that, wasn't his problem really only a microcosm revealing a brand-new opportunity 3M could create for people at work—an easy way to secure and remove reminders and notes that could eliminate one more thing for people to remember and act on?

Directly experiencing a problem or opportunity that is either existing but unexplored or newly emerging is one way that people and organizations uncover a nondisruptive opportunity. Leaders here pay acute attention, pause, and lean into their direct experience. They don't simply write it off. Instead, they actively register it, alertly focus on it, and don't let it go as they think deeply about the real difference addressing it would make to the world. If the potential impact is great and the market potential is of a magnitude that they deem to be meaningful, they consciously set out to explore it with an intent to deliver.

Remember the taken-for-granted problem that Jack Dorsey and Jim McKelvey set out to solve with the Square Reader: individuals and microbusinesses were losing sales because they couldn't accept credit card payments. It was McKelvey's direct loss of a sale for his glassblowing business that raised the existing but unexplored problem to his and Dorsey's consciousness and made them passionate about solving it as they appreciated how many could benefit from this new market. Likewise, Bette Nesmith Graham hated having to retype an entire page every time she made a typing error. Instead of metaphorically shrugging her shoulders and seeing retyping as simply a downside of being a secretary (as in fact countless secretaries did), she set out to solve this existing but unexplored problem with her Mistake Out that led to Liquid Paper.

What existing but taken-for-granted problems do you or your company directly experience that no industry exists to solve? What newly emerging issues are you or your organization encountering that could create a real opportunity for you or your business, but no industry exists to address them?

Empathetically observing

A second way to identify a nondisruptive opportunity is to pay acute attention to an existing problem that is unexplored or newly emerging and that leaders *indirectly* experience by empathetically observing.

Bilikiss Adebiyi-Abiola, who founded Wecyclers, was born in Lagos, Nigeria, and had been living in the United States for several years, where she had worked as a software engineer at IBM. While visiting her family back home, she was struck by the stark contrast in the quality of life for the more than 10 million people living in Lagos's slums, where the streets were littered with trash, and the residents were cut off from any form of municipal garbage collection. Adebiyi-Abiola had no direct experience of living in Lagos's slum conditions. To the contrary, she had attended a prominent secondary school in Lagos before moving to the United States. Yet when she went home, the blight jumped out at her. Feeling pain for those people, she identified a nondisruptive opportunity to turn the slums' trash into cash through recycling, thereby cleaning the streets, creating jobs, and putting extra money in the hands of the poor.

Or recall how Pfizer spotted the nondisruptive opportunity that became Viagra. The research team was conducting trials on a drug for blood pressure treatment. But in the process of gathering feedback from the people in the trial, they discovered something surprising and unexpected. As one man shared, the drug triggered more erections during the night. The nodding agreements in the room that the researchers observed spoke volumes. This is how Pfizer saw (and heard) the possibility of a nondisruptive opportunity it could create with a market solution for ED. And it knew that no one was addressing this issue.

And when Lloyd Morrisett, a cofounder of the Children's Television Workshop, woke up one morning to find his preschool daughter watching test patterns on the television, something clicked in his mind. He started to investigate whether TV could open a brand-new opportunity to educate preschool children across America. As he shared his observation and thoughts with Joan Ganz Cooney, a PBS programmer at the time, she started to closely observe how young children interacted with TV. She saw that they not only were mesmerized by it, but effortlessly memorized and recited back all the commercial jingles popular on TV in those days. That's when Morrisett and Cooney, the eventual cocreators of Sesame Street, saw the potential nondisruptive opportunity of using television as a medium for preschool children across America.

What existing or newly emerging issues do you or your company observe that could create a real threat or opportunity for you, your business, or people, but that no industry exists to address?

Actively scouting

A third way to identify a nondisruptive opportunity is to purposefully look for one. Mick Ebeling, the founder of Not Impossible Labs, and his team actively scout out problems or opportunities that are seen as impossible to solve and are in line with the labs' core value of "technology for the sake of humanity." They tap into all their direct and indirect contacts, networks, and communications, and also visit action sites for exploration as needed. That's how Ebeling identified the nondisruptive opportunities that became Project Daniel and Music: Not Impossible.

Not Impossible Labs also assiduously scouts brand-new problems or opportunities, especially medically related ones, by inviting people to submit them. If a submission resonates with the Not Impossible Labs team and aligns with their core value, and they believe that a solution could make a real difference, the team sets out to create a market solution. As Ebeling says, "Everything that today is possible was once viewed as impossible. Just as what appears impossible today is on a trajectory to being made possible. If it is worthwhile and we are passionate about it, we explore *Why not now; why not by us?*"[2]

Are you actively scouting brand-new problems to solve and brand-new opportunities to create that no industry exists to address? Do you have a mechanism or a process for achieving this effectively?

Assessing and Framing the Opportunity
for the Next Step

Before moving on to the second building block, you should take two actions. The first is to ask, Who other than you cares about this problem or opportunity? What are the market potential and the impact potential of the nondisruptive opportunity you have identified? Market and impact potentials need to be assessed in terms of both economic gain and wider benefits for society. This assessment will help you see whether the opportunity you've identified is a likely candidate to meet your objective or purpose.

The second action is to frame the opportunity in a grounded and motivating way. If it's framed too broadly, you might be overwhelmed by its breadth and lose focus. To ensure that the opportunity you are pursuing is deemed to be within your reach and realizable, especially at the start, you need to frame it in a way that you and your team can envision its feasibility and are inspired to take it on with confidence.

Let's look at how nondisruptive creators tackle these actions.

Who cares besides you? Assess the size
of the potential market

Like the founders of the nondisruptive markets we've detailed, you want to be sure that the opportunity you have identified is not just a burning issue for you. It should be an issue that has real relevance to others and thus has true market and impact potential. In other words, you want to be clear on who truly cares other than you. You should assess the size of its potential market up front, before you pour in your time and resources.

Jack Dorsey and Jim McKelvey knew that the nondisruptive opportunity they were setting out to solve with the Square Reader was personal to McKelvey and other small merchants he knew. The question was, How big was the market potential? How many other people were likely to seriously care? The two set out to answer this question and found that millions of small merchants, not to mention microbusinesses and the self-employed, saw no way to accept credit cards, the overwhelmingly dominant form of payment. This puts them at a clear disadvantage compared with larger merchants when it came to ease of sales. The problem, in short, wasn't just that of McKelvey and his friends. The market potential was huge if solved.

In setting out to understand the plight of the poor in Bangladesh, Mohammad Yunus discovered to his amazement that a loan of as little as twenty-two cents could change the life of one impoverished Bangladeshi woman. That sum was a very far cry from the hundreds of millions of dollars that development agencies often kick around to make even a small dent in poverty. Yunus launched a project with his students to study the Jobra district directly outside his university to see how prevalent the problem was. In going door-to-door, he found that strikingly half the total population of the district was earning so little by weaving baskets, sifting rice, or making sleeping mats that they had absolutely no chance of improving their economic circumstances. Having extrapolated this to all of Bangladesh, Yunus could see that the market for loans in the single digits that could change lives was enormous.

The nondisruptive opportunity you have identified needn't promise to touch and be relevant to as many people as those that led to the Square Reader, Grameen Bank, or Sesame Street. What matters is your organization's size and ambitions and what you are passionate about. Nondisruptive creation can be large or small. Music:

Not Impossible opened a nondisruptive new market, but not on a scale anywhere close to that for e-sports. Only you can determine what is right for you and your company. Your impact can be great even in small ways. Nevertheless, you should check that others will value the nondisruptive opportunity you have identified. If your ambition is big, you need to check that the number of those struggling from it or who could benefit by it in a meaningful way is large. And if your ambition is smaller, you need to check that the problem or opportunity you aim to address will deliver compelling value for the select population you imagine it for.

Dream big, but start small. Use atomization to frame the identified opportunity

To follow through on the creation journey, it's crucial not only to assess the size of the market potential, but also to atomize the challenge for you and your team so that you are not overwhelmed and ultimately demotivated by the breadth of the problem or opportunity. When a challenge appears enormous, it can also appear unsolvable—especially if your resources are limited. That can quickly demotivate the team and make it too easy to quit. You can also lose focus.

Not Impossible Labs didn't try to solve the existing but unexplored problem of all amputees in Sudan or other war-torn countries, for that matter. Instead the team atomized it to "Let's create arms for Daniel so that he can feed himself." That was far more personal and humanizing. The cofounders of Prodigy Finance didn't set out to solve cross-border financing for global advanced education— although they ended up doing just that. Initially, they atomized it to "Let's solve cross-border funding for prospective INSEAD students" so that they could get their minds around the challenge, and it felt far more doable and personal. Likewise, Mohammad Yunus didn't set out to solve extreme poverty all across Bangladesh. He knew the immensity of the challenge wouldn't be credible. People on his team would just roll their eyes and think, *Oh yeah, sure*. To be taken seriously and inspire his team, he atomized the challenge so that people could imagine creating a market solution for it by starting microloans in one village.

Essentially, atomizing your nondisruptive opportunity makes it much more mentally attainable. It frames the challenge on a more human scale that effectively relaxes us so that our minds can go to work and not be frozen like a deer in headlights by the scope of what we set out to create. When you cast the nondisruptive opportunity as too broad, it can immediately become daunting. People don't know where to start and can easily lose their way. But if you atomize it—no matter how large it may be—it starts to look achievable. And it creates a far more relatable story, which is what you want as you move on to the second building block.

In the next chapter, we dive into building block two. That's where we lay out what process and tools you can apply to find a way to unlock the nondisruptive opportunity you have identified.

Chapter Eight

Find a Way to Unlock
the Opportunity

Once you've identified a nondisruptive opportunity and properly assessed and framed it, the next step is to find a way to unlock it. The best way to achieve this begins with understanding why and how the opportunity has been overlooked or gone unaddressed. That means unearthing the existing assumptions that have concealed the opportunity and then challenging and reframing them to capture it. The existing assumptions here mean the current assumptions held by the industry to which your identified nondisruptive opportunity would seem to naturally belong but doesn't. The question to answer here is: What industry should theoretically address this issue, and why hasn't it done so?

Our research shows that nondisruptive opportunities have often been overlooked because of the relevant industry's conventional

FIGURE 8-1

The assumption-implication framework

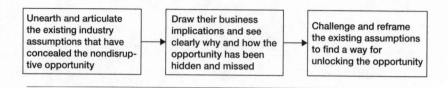

assumptions regarding its business model: in particular, how the risk-return of the business is assessed, who its target customers are, and what the scope of the business is. Once you draw the business implications of those conventional assumptions, the reasons why and how the opportunity has been hidden and missed will start to come into focus, so you can challenge and reframe them to find a way to unlock the opportunity. Figure 8-1 provides an overview of how this process works.

Unearth the Assumptions That Have Concealed the Opportunity

To discover the assumptions concealing the opportunity and draw out their business implications in a more structured way, we introduce a tool, the assumption-implication analysis. The assumption-implication analysis is a one-page analytic that will help you identify and unpack the implicit and explicit assumptions of the industry that should have spotted and acted on the opportunity you've found but didn't. The key assumptions to analyze relate to the core elements of the industry's business model: risk-return assessment, target customers, and business scope. As you conduct such an analysis, you will not only discover why those assumptions have concealed the opportunity from the existing industry but also see how you can challenge them to unlock it.

Take Prodigy Finance. The nondisruptive opportunity that it identified was financing education loans for advanced degrees abroad. Even though corporations increasingly seek to hire global talent with advanced degrees and international exposure, students couldn't get the funding to earn advanced degrees overseas—especially at top universities, where tuition is notably steep. This applies to students seeking master's degrees in other countries, whether in business, engineering, law, or public administration.

The industry that should theoretically have addressed this burning but unaddressed problem is banking. Although the number of international students had grown by more than 200 percent over the previous two decades alone, traditional banks were oblivious to the burgeoning demand for overseas-study loans. Why? What were the long-held assumptions that blocked players in the industry from seeing and addressing this nondisruptive opportunity?

To answer that question, Prodigy had to peel back banking's assumptions and their implications under two scenarios: one is when prospective students seek financing from banks in their home countries, and the other is when students seek it from a bank in the host country of their international study.

Table 8-1 outlines the assumption-implication analysis for overseas education loans from the vantage point of the existing banking industry. That industry saw those loans as a business beyond the industry's scope or boundary. As seen in the table, the first column lays out the three key elements of a business model: how the risk-return of the business is assessed, who are the target customers for the business, and what is the position of the business relative to its overall business scope. The next two columns detail what Prodigy

TABLE 8-1

The assumption-implication analysis

For overseas education loans

Existing banking industry	Assumptions	Implications
Risk-return assessment (loan requirements)	Good *domestic* credit report and employment history are needed for loans; absent these, *domestic* collateral or a guarantor is needed; the future return expected from an overseas study is unknown; financing it without having the loan requirements met is extremely risky and undoable.	Most foreign students have no access to an overseas loan as they cannot meet the loan requirements; overseas education is mostly self-financed or family-funded; unless the future return expected from foreign study can be measured and somewhat certain, the loan requirements will be strictly imposed.
Target customers	For education loans, citizens and permanent residents are the main target customers; for overseas education loans, even among citizens and permanent residents, only those with the needed financial credentials are potential customers to consider.	It is impossible for foreign students with a student visa to get a loan for their education in the host countries of their study; it is not easy to get a foreign study loan in their home countries either; the foreign-study loan seekers are not the main target customers of banks.
Business scope	The business from overseas study loans can only be marginal.	Overseas study loans are not within the scope of banks' main business.

discovered as it fleshed out the key assumptions of conventional banks and the corresponding business implications of those assumptions for each of the three elements.

As Prodigy put together what it found, it realized that the banking industry had remained essentially localized since its founding. In fact, the word *bank* itself can be traced to eighteenth-century Italy, where traders sat on benches (*banca*) in local markets to lend money to local borrowers. Modern banks kept to this tradition of lending only to local parties because they believed it was essential for mitigating default risk: these borrowers had domestic collateral to put up against their loans, and banks could properly assess their creditworthiness based on their identity, local job history, and credit record.

Even though the mobility of capital, goods, and human beings was greatly enhanced during the era of globalization, banks staunchly retained the local basis of their personal-loan business. Their implicit and explicit assumptions about how the educational-loan business should be tackled were rooted in such conventional, localized practice.

As the table shows, banks make several assumptions regarding the risk-return on education loans. They assume that a strong local credit report is necessary to ascertain an applicant's creditworthiness and intent to repay. A foreign credit history is considered suspect and irrelevant because it originates outside the home country and is perceived as difficult to verify and make sense of. Banks also assume that a solid employment history and a job of good standing they can easily verify are equally important evidence of creditworthiness and low default risk. But to be easily verifiable, jobs, incomes, and employment histories must be domestically based. Absent that, a bank will demand local collateral in considerable excess of the requested loan amount and/or a local cosigner to guarantee the loan. Recall how HSBC, the one bank that did discuss financing options with Cameron Stevens, a cofounder of Prodigy, had asked him to put up 100 percent of liquid assets to lend him only 75 percent of the money. Put another way, only an applicant's track record and current assets are treated as valid bases for education-loan approval, and they must be domestically based.

Banks' target customers for education loans are citizens or permanent residents, not foreign nationals with temporary student visas. That's because foreign students have a mismatch between their temporary stay and the longer-term nature of education loans, creating a perceived flight risk for banks. Even citizens and long-term residents must still pass the banks' creditworthiness criteria to be considered for education loans.

In terms of business scope, banks focus on financing education loans designated for domestic or local use. They view financing loans for study in a foreign country as high risk, because cross-border legal recourse is both difficult and costly and is outside their business purview. Hence overseas-study loans are highly discouraged and not within the scope of their main business.

Understand the Business Implications for Why the Opportunity Was Missed

The implications of these long-accepted assumptions and practices were drawn out and clear. As seen in table 8-1, banks in host countries were not interested in extending loans to international students, because these students have no permanent residence, no local credit record, no local employment history, and no local collateral with which to establish creditworthiness. And almost all lack upstanding local cosigners to act as guarantors of their repayment.

Back in the home countries of those students, financial institutions were equally preoccupied with the domestic loan business. Existing education-loan products were designed for students who pursued education at home. These banks treated loans for pursuing advanced degrees abroad as outside their main scope of business and exceptionally high risk. Banks assess loans according to historical data and current assets, and most international students are relatively young, with neither rich credit and employment histories nor significant local collateral to justify the large amounts required to finance top-tier postgraduate education abroad. There is also the perceived added risk that students might choose to stay abroad after their study, making recourse for loan defaults legally challenging and expensive.

The upshot is that the home-country banks of prospective students were typically unwilling to discuss loans for postgraduate study abroad. And in cases when they were willing, major collateral was required and interest rates were horrendously high—above 30 percent in some countries. Loan applicants could also expect mountains of paperwork, only to receive a fraction of the amount they needed for tuition. As shown in the table, most overseas graduate study was self-financed, like Stevens's, or family funded. When neither of those options was possible, students might have to defer their studies for years while they accumulated the funds or simply give up their dream altogether. Understandably, students from emerging and developing economies were affected disproportionately because of the disparity in income levels between these countries and more advanced economies, where the vast majority of top-tier, high-cost, advanced-degree programs reside.

Reframe the Assumptions to Unlock the Opportunity

Armed with this understanding, Prodigy challenged and reframed the banking industry's assumptions to develop an alternative model for financing overseas graduate study. It started with the risk-return assessment. As INSEAD students themselves, the company's founders knew that regardless of how little assets or income or credit history students might have accumulated before entry, one thing was certain: statistics showed that upon graduation from a top-tier business school like INSEAD, a student's salary, on average, would receive a significant boost and often would double, landing mostly in the six-figure range. What's more, graduates of INSEAD and other top-tier MBA programs would most likely receive multiple job offers from leading companies across the globe. So their earning potential, far from being "uncertain," as banks assumed, was virtually certain and would place graduates in the tier of high-income earners.

Prodigy also reflected on what it takes to gain admittance to a leading graduate school like INSEAD: students had to have excellent undergraduate grades, high test scores, and impressive nonacademic achievements such as leadership roles in clubs or sports to get in. Accordingly, Prodigy asked, weren't these all robust, proven, and telling measures of the discipline, determination, and follow-through the students would bring to their financial commitments? Would people who had invested that much effort to gain admittance and to get prestigious positions upon graduation be so cavalier as to risk everything by not repaying their debt? On the contrary, wouldn't they be extremely conscientious in building their credit, repaying their loans, and compounding their success? Prodigy reasoned that if it could secure data on the stature and reputation of the university and the advanced-degree program that a student had been admitted to and on its postgraduation income and job statistics, it would have the basis for developing a new model of international students' creditworthiness and default risk that was far more accurate than the students' pre-graduate-school salary level and credit data.

Prodigy understood that legal recourse and enforceability was a main reason that banks stuck to domestic education loans. But, it reasoned, why—in this global, highly connected world—couldn't it create a global enforceability infrastructure? Sure, credit can be

it safer to increase the number of existing domestic cricket matches that were aligned with this tradition.

Accordingly, BCCI's target customers were cricket purists who revered the nobility and conservatism of the old-world sport and its traditional matches, in which players' strength, competence, and perseverance were tested over the games' long duration.

As for business scope, existing national and regional league matches played by domestic players were the sport's key revenue source. BCCI's business goal was managing them to maximize ticket sales and event sponsorship.

These long-accepted assumptions and their implications can be seen in table 8-2. Essentially, BCCI's focus on international standards and tradition led it to overlook the modernizing, far more dynamic and shortened Twenty20 game format, introduced by the England and Wales Cricket Board in 2003, which slashed matches from days to three hours, making cricket events fast paced and far easier to attend. In catering to hard-core cricket fans, BCCI missed the importance of fun and thrills: traditional matches were too long and too slow for non-hard-core members of the public to justify committing days to attend them. Furthermore, the long-match formats were ill-suited for TV viewing, so they missed out on widespread TV viewership and lucrative sponsorship revenue.

Armed with the understanding of these implications, BCCI, with Modi's push, reframed the existing assumptions to envisage a way to create an entirely new business—"cricketainment"—and a new league, built on the three-hour Twenty20 format for fast action and accompanied by dancing, music, fireworks, and light shows, and importantly open to international cricketeers as well as Indians, for a high level of play, glamour, and international cachet. By franchising the new league's teams and setting them up as for-profit rather than nonprofit, BCCI saw a way to draw in tycoons, Bollywood

TABLE 8-2

The assumption-implication analysis

For cricket in India

BCCI under old leadership	Assumptions	Implications
Risk-return assessment	The mission is to honor and cherish the tradition of cricket in India; respecting the tradition, only Indians could play on India's teams; preserve classic several-day or one-day game format; as a nonprofit public organization, deviations from these traditional practices for growth are risky as they can be seen as commercially driven moves, tarnishing the image; to boost return and revenue it is safer to increase the number of existing cricket matches that are aligned with the tradition.	The modernizing opportunity for adopting more dynamic and entertaining cricket games based on the fast-paced three-hour Twenty20 game format with international players is missed; as the long matches are ill-suited to TV coverage, the opportunities for attracting wider cricket viewers and earning big revenues from TV broadcasting are missed; with limited growth and returns, Indian players are paid lower than their international counterparts.
Target customers	Indian diehard cricket fans support traditional values of the sport; the aim is to expand the base of such core fans for the growth of cricket in India while keeping up its original tradition.	The opportunity for broadening the cricket customer base is missed by not offering nontraditional values such as fun and thrill that could appeal to general Indians, the majority in the nation, who currently are cricket noncustomers.
Business scope	Existing national and regional league matches performed by domestic players are key revenue sources; the business goal is managing them to maximize their ticket sales and event sponsorships.	The opportunity for expanding the existing business scope is missed; with the media-friendly short matches played by international stars, cricket could widen its revenue streams by having mass appeal.

stars, entrepreneurs, and other celebrities to become team owners, which would not only add to the new league's aura, but also give each team deep pockets with which to secure and compensate top Indian and international cricketeers for great play—all the while dropping BCCI's cost structure.

Exciting short matches would appeal to all demographics and would be ideal for attending events and wide TV viewership with lucrative TV sponsorship. And because BCCI is the sport's governing body in India, it could coordinate the new league's schedules to avoid conflict with the dates of existing domestic and international matches—making it literally impossible for viewers (or cricketeers) to make any trade-offs with existing cricket league matches.

With its launch of the Indian Premier League (IPL), BCCI created the nondisruptive new market of cricketainment. Since its first year, in 2008, IPL has received an overwhelming response: matches are sold out, and TV viewership has been estimated at 200 million Indians plus 10 million overseas viewers. As of 2021, IPL was valued at about $6 billion, with its viewership climbing to more than 400 million. With the creation of IPL, BCCI transformed its flat growth line into a steep upward trajectory as it spread the passion for cricket and inspired sports-inclined youths to join in and play at the top of the sport.

The Importance of Thinking for Yourself and Being Prepared for Pundits

In conducting an assumption-implication analysis, you will want to bear two points in mind. One is not to fall into the trap of taking the assumptions of others as your own. The other is to prepare for discouragement from the pundits.

Don't take on others' assumptions

Have the courage to develop an independent point of view and to openly question. When Joan Ganz Cooney, a cocreator of Sesame

Street, presented the brand-new idea of preschool edutainment, experts in the education industry—to which this opportunity seemed to naturally belong—held different assumptions. They stemmed from their existing theories that mixing fantasy (think Muppets) with reality would likely confuse children and should be avoided; that for preschoolers to learn, they must *do* things—not merely *see* them (as on TV); that teachers, rather than fuzzy make-believe animals, are the best educators; and that young children have very short attention spans—which is true when educational materials are didactically taught, but not, as Cooney's reframing found, when learning is wrapped in fantasy, music, and story.

Sesame Street's approach was antithetical to the education industry at the time. In using humor, song, and animation to attract and hold children's attention, it seemed more like commercial television. Just as TV advertisers use commercials to sell products, Sesame Street used jingles and repetition to teach numbers and letters in a way that no one had ever imagined before.

Get ready for discouragement from the pundits

Education experts and government officials were intrigued but initially cast doubt and skepticism on the nondisruptive opportunity that Joan Ganz Cooney and Lloyd Morrisett had identified. Even at the US Office of Education, many seemed initially disdainful of the idea of educational television at all, with many even viewing it as "mind-numbing, arch, and amateurish."[2] That it could capture and hold young children's attention—let alone that they could ever learn from it—was doubted. Cameron Stevens and his Prodigy Finance cofounders were strongly urged to abandon the nondisruptive opportunity they'd identified with a common refrain: *It's not possible.* The reasons they were given ranged from "Finance is too heavily regulated" to "If banks can't do cross-border lending, then how can you?" to "Everyone knows that past data, not future potential, is how credit is assessed." And Mohammad Yunus was told that the nondisruptive opportunity he'd identified was damned from the get-go. The banking community and government officials laughed at the idea and patronized him. So be ready to face discouragement from the pundits.

When you expect discouragement, you're far less likely to be discouraged when it comes. Equally important, you'll better retain the equanimity you need to wisely assess whether any valuable learning lies in the pundits' refrain. Did they raise an important issue that you overlooked? Could this strengthen your idea about how to unlock the opportunity? Did they shed light on a hidden complexity you had missed for why the opportunity had gone unaddressed that you should reassess in your reframing? View criticism not as a dagger but as a way to stress-test your idea, learn, and strengthen your path forward.

With this understanding, in the next chapter we explore the third building block, where we discuss both how to realize the opportunity and the dance between competence and confidence needed to succeed.

Chapter Nine

Realize the Opportunity

O nce you've identified a nondisruptive opportunity to pursue and found a way to unlock it, the next step is to realize it. This third and final building block aims to help you achieve this in a high-value, low-cost way. In this chapter, we first lay out the key enablers you need and discuss how to secure them. We then show how you can ensure that the people involved are intellectually and emotionally behind the opportunity and are committed to act on and realize it.

Figure 9-1 presents an overall framework that depicts the key action steps across the three building blocks for achieving nondisruptive creation. As shown, the process starts with identifying a nondisruptive opportunity (the first building block) and finding a way to unlock it (the second building block). The opportunity can be either existing but unexplored or newly emerging outside existing industry boundaries. The process then moves on to the third

FIGURE 9-1

A framework for realizing nondisruptive creation

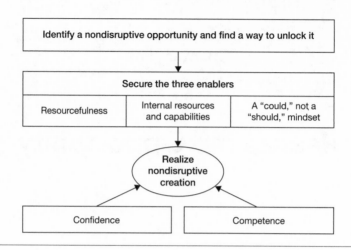

building block, where we discuss the three enablers essential to make the opportunity happen—resourcefulness, internal resources and capabilities, and a "could" rather than "should" mindset—and how to secure them. There you can learn how to capture the opportunity in a high-value, low-cost way. The process ends with a tool that can help you assess and see if your approach is on track to succeed or needs to be modified and further developed. The tool is built on two elements: your people's collective confidence in the opportunity and their competence to pull it off.

The Three Enablers

Resourcefulness

Resourcefulness reflects the adage "The world is your oyster." It is the ability to creatively leverage the world's constellation of knowledge, expertise, resources, and capabilities, even without owning them, to deliver what is needed to realize the nondisruptive opportunity you have identified. It allows you to achieve way beyond what you could accomplish using only your own resources and capabilities—and to do so at lower cost, with less capital, and often with greater expertise and speed than you could on your own.

Resourcefulness has several elements, starting with Googling or DuckDuckGoing what you're struggling to figure out. Instead of thinking, *We don't know or have the expertise to figure this out*, find out who does or might know so that you can learn everything about it. There's a whole world of free knowledge and education out there for anyone to take advantage of, though many people and organizations don't. It has never been easier to do your own research and find answers. At no cost you can learn sales techniques from a podcast; how to use 3D printing for mass manufacturing on YouTube; coding from Khan Academy; design; sourcing; finance; packaging; and taxation and regulations across countries, states, or counties. Never underestimate the wealth of knowledge, education, and informative podcasts, videos, and digital articles available to you free on almost any subject—from the technical to the scientific to the metaphysical, including from the foremost thinkers and doers across fields—which you can skillfully leverage to realize your nondisruptive opportunity and make yourself an expert.

When Mick Ebeling, Daniel Belquer, and Not Impossible Labs set out to realize Music: Not Impossible, Belquer, a technical music artist, searched out scientific studies on vibration, the auditory functioning of the ear, and the neurological transmission that occurs between the brain, the ear, and the skin. Although Belquer himself is not a scientist, a brain specialist, or a doctor of audiology, nor is Ebeling, through resourcefulness they were able to leverage, essentially at no cost, the best knowledge out there to both understand the clues on how to make Music: Not Impossible possible and actually overcome obstacles as they built it.

In Prodigy Finance's case, Cameron Stevens was no expert on global loan enforcement or legal recourse for defaults in foreign countries. Yet after he and his cofounders identified them as key pillars in building a robust business model for their company, they used their resourcefulness, including learning from local credit best practices and the internet to find out all they could on the underlying rules governing credit behavior in countries and regions (despite the apparent differences), to pioneer a framework for global loan enforceability. Stevens and his partners didn't start out as experts in this area, but they became experts.

What knowledge do you lack or need a deeper understanding of to realize your nondisruptive opportunity? Make a list of whatever it is and start searching the internet. Begin with broad parameters to cast your knowledge net wide. Then narrow your search as you gain clarity on the specifics you need to zoom in on and which key players may have them.

Resourcefulness embraces another element, which is purposefully looking to other industries, other fields, or parallel situations now or in the past to identify clues and creative practices that might be applied to realize your nondisruptive creation. In the case of Kickstarter, Perry Chen, Yancey Strickler, and Charles Adler looked far back in time to understand how artists had historically gotten their work funded. They found that it wasn't simply a matter of the Medici family or the Church coming in to fund artistic work. In a number of instances, a large audience had funded a creative work—such as Alexander Pope's translation of the *Iliad* from Greek to English. For that endeavor, 750 people provided funding and in return got their names inscribed in the first edition. That was an important clue to how Kickstarter could get around monetary incentives for funders and instead offer rewards such as name recognition on an artist's website.

Likewise, to realize Sesame Street, Joan Ganz Cooney borrowed practices from the advertising industry—from songs to color to speed to alliteration—to hold kids' attention and get ideas to stick in their minds. And the gaming industry looked to worldwide sports to gain insight into how to realize e-sports leagues and host global e-sports championship competitions, including how to create the hype, get the word out, and monetize the competitions through broadcast licensing.

What other industries, domains, analogous situations, or points in time might offer insights into how to go about realizing your nondisruptive creation? Think freely and broadly as you answer this question to find innovative ideas or ways to overcome the hurdles you confront and fill in the missing pieces of the nondisruptive puzzle you set out to solve.

A third element of resourcefulness is recognizing the resources, talents, technological expertise, and capabilities held outside your organization or existing team and leveraging them through formal or informal partnerships. For Music: Not Impossible, Mick Ebeling reached out to Mandy Harvey, the profoundly deaf American pop singer, to bring a perspective no one on the team at Not Impossible Labs had on how skin vibrations on different parts of the body correspond to a sense of sound, whether more sensors were needed, and what intensity and vibration would effectively trigger the experience of music when transmitted from the skin to the brain for the deaf. Ebeling also partnered with Avnet, leveraging its deep technology expertise to help refine and manufacture Music: Not Impossible's sleek, lightweight, and comfortable vibro-techno vest.

Or take Prodigy Finance. It formally partnered with top universities to gain direct access to their deep databases of graduates' job placement, salary outcomes, career trajectories, test scores, and more, which allowed it to build a credible new risk-return assessment model based on students' future earning potential. The universities were motivated to share that proprietary information because Prodigy made a solid case for how its new nondisruptive market would make their advanced-degree programs more accessible to foreign students, with accepted foreign nationals ultimately more likely to also join because of its funding.

Likewise think of Square. To create the nondisruptive market of credit card payments for microbusinesses and individuals, Jim McKelvey and Jack Dorsey essentially leveraged—at virtually no cost—all the research and development that went into Apple's iPhone.[1] How's that? When they determined that a key component of their nondisruptive creation was a small, unencumbered device that people could carry with them and use anywhere to process credit card payments, McKelvey started looking outside for what he could leverage.[2] He observed that the iPhone could act as a newspaper, a TV, a camera, a map, a photo album, and even a stereo. So why couldn't Square leverage the inherent technology in this device to process credit cards? And that's exactly what Square did. The Square Reader, which allows you to swipe your credit card for payment, plugs straight into the headphone jack on the iPhone and on all other smartphones as well. And because the headphone jack is a universal and open standard, Square didn't need to partner with or pay Apple for the use of this brilliant device. In this way, what could easily have been a costly element of its nondisruptive creation to build came at a price tag of near to zero for Square.

Who from outside your organization do you need to bring in to realize your nondisruptive solution? Where could you get the resources you lack? Which organization or organizations have the technical expertise or capabilities you need? Leveraging the expertise, capabilities, and economies of scale of outside individuals and companies can substantially pare down your costs and close any capability gaps you may have.

A last element of resourcefulness is unearthing and leveraging existing but unused or underutilized social capital to realize your nondisruptive creation. "Social capital" refers to the norms, understandings, bonds, and mutual commitments of people who live in a particular society or community. To get around the fact that the extremely poor are illiterate and have no collateral, Mohammad Yunus leveraged their tight social bonds to ensure that loans were repaid and that the funds borrowed were used for productive means to help break the cycle of poverty.

To get a loan, five villagers must come together to form a mutually supportive unit. Then the bank will extend a tiny loan to one member designated by the group. Only if that person regularly repays the loan for several months can another member of the group request a loan. This creates not-so-subtle peer pressure for no member to default and naturally incentivizes groups to select only members who feel a sense of kinship and a high moral obligation to not let the other members down. The codependence also inspires members to step up and help any member of the group who may be struggling, making each borrower more reliable in the process.

By uncovering and leveraging existing but unutilized social capital, Grameen Bank not only made financial capital accessible for the first time to the extremely poor but also achieved a 98 percent repayment rate. Furthermore, it took the costs attached to loan approval, enforcement, collection, and contracts down significantly.

For Compte-Nickel, a key challenge was how to distribute its bank-in-a-box to the five million unbankable people of France in an effective and low-cost way. To address this challenge, the company sought to identify places that those people could be expected to feel socially comfortable in and visit frequently. It found the answer in interesting places: tabacs and news agencies, where locals gather daily to chat and purchase frequent needs, such as newspapers, tobacco products, stamps, lottery tickets, and mobile phone rechargers. These outlets offered a special social space for the unbanked and many other French people.

Tabacs and news agencies already had a pervasive footprint all over France, with very long operating hours and availability in even the most remote and rural locations. Compte-Nickel partnered with them to distribute its low-cost basic bank account. Best yet, given the prime locations of these outlets and the frequency of people's visits there, Compte-Nickel achieved rapid brand awareness and sales from word of mouth alone, with no advertising expense.

Instead of looking only to market-based economic means to realize your nondisruptive creation, ask, Is there social capital we can leverage? What social norms, established bonds of trust (like those La Poste workers had with citizens in France), mutual commitments, or high-level aligned interests (like those Mick Ebeling drew on to realize Music: Not Impossible) might you leverage?

Internal resources and capabilities

Realizing nondisruptive opportunities also rests on the resources and capabilities that organizations already possess and those they build or acquire. Rarely can you simply leverage everything from outside, through formal or informal partnerships—nor would you necessarily want to. Here you want to look to your tangible resources and capabilities, such as technology, capital, R&D or manufacturing facilities, and other physical assets, and also the intangible ones that are encoded in your organization's and team's knowledge and know-how: design, miniaturization, coding, social influence, teamwork, brand awareness, among others.

How can you realize your nondisruptive opportunity by leveraging internal assets in a way that achieves high value at a low cost? Can you creatively combine internal resources and capabilities to realize the opportunity in an effective and efficient way? And how can you leverage your organization's or team's existing knowledge and skills to build or creatively acquire what you need?

Let's revisit the Tongwei Group, long a leader in China's aquaculture industry. In the mid-2000s, the group diversified into the manufacturing of polysilicon, an essential material for solar panels. When, in the early 2010s, China declared its ambition to cap carbon emissions by 2030, there was a surge in the building of green-energy production facilities in western China, where land was abundant—but not where it was most needed. That was in the provinces of eastern and central China, where industrial activities were concentrated, and power demand was high and rising fast. In those densely populated regions, land that was suitable for green-energy facilities was scarce, because most of it was mandated for agricultural use by the government. What those regions did have was lots of water, much of it used for fish farming.

Because of its role in the aquaculture industry, Tongwei was very familiar with fish farms, their locations, and their water characteristics. And it had built strong relationships and partnerships with the regions' fish farmers and local governing bodies—resources that few other companies had. Instead of viewing the fish farms as limited to its aquaculture business, Tongwei saw that it could leverage and effectively repurpose its knowledge and relationships to deliver a brand-new nondisruptive opportunity of green energy for these regions.

Creatively combining its expertise in fish-farm water bodies, industrialized aquaculture, and solar energy, Tongwei designed an innovative way to integrate PV solar panels with aquaculture waters that was not only technically feasible but would provide added income for the fish farmers and tax revenues to local governments while creating a brand-new growth horizon and business for the company: Tongwei New Energy. All that was required from the fish farmers and the local governing bodies was agreement that Tongwei be able to rent and take advantage of the unused water surfaces. Tongwei Group effectively multiplied fish farmers' yield below the water's surface with aquaculture and delivered green energy for the state above it. The result was a win for everyone that was nondisruptive to industry.

Tongwei achieved its success by creatively combining and leveraging largely internal resources and capabilities. But as we've noted, a nondisruptive opportunity can also be realized by building new resources and capabilities and combining them with those you already have. Consider how Ping An Insurance, a Chinese *Fortune* 500 company, realized the multibillion-dollar nondisruptive opportunity of primary health care in China. Whereas quality health care is well established in Western countries, that was not the case in China, where access to it was a long-unresolved problem given the absence of any system of publicly recognized private doctors or independent general practitioners.

Historically, whatever health problems or concerns the Chinese had, they trusted only the leading public hospitals and the well-credentialed doctors employed there. The issue was that nearly 50 percent of the people going to big public hospitals shouldn't have gone there in the first place, because they went to consult doctors on minor problems or general or chronic conditions when the doctors there were highly specialized and already overloaded. The result was massively overburdened public hospitals, doctors who saw more than one hundred patients a day, and a poor patient experience with consultation time only a few minutes. That led people, especially those from smaller cities or remote rural areas, to often choose to self-diagnose or seek help from unlicensed clinics, resulting in misdiagnoses and incurring serious consequences for patients' health.

To address this existing but unresolved and unexplored problem, Ping An leveraged its strong reputation and deep pockets of capital to establish Ping An Good Doctor, granting it brand recognition and funds. But to realize the nondisruptive market, Ping An Good Doctor needed a network of highly credentialed doctors whom the Chinese people would trust and be open to using. Because the only doctors they currently trusted were already employed and overworked in the country's select few highest-ranked hospitals, partnering or a referral system wouldn't work.

To get around this, Ping An saw a possibility: it could build a comparable team of full-time doctors who had all served in top hospitals but had left for various professional or personal reasons. It turns out that competition among doctors was intense inside the best hospitals. Moving up the career ladder required not only excellent medical skills and performance but also a strong research record, because research was one of the key criteria in grading hospitals. Doctors who were experienced in practice but had less ambition or interest in research were sometimes motivated by peer pressure and dim prospects for promotion to quit their jobs and seek opportunities elsewhere. These aspiring doctors would not seek employment with a lower-level medical institution or start an independent practice, because those were not mainstream options in the Chinese social setting. So these doctors would rather drop out of medicine and take up another health-related profession, such as working as a sales rep for a major pharmaceutical company, although that would mean wasting their previous investment in clinical training.

Ping An saw this pool of top doctors as an overlooked resource it could bring in-house. It offered them a promising opportunity to stay in medical practice and be part of a brand-new cause while earning good pay and stock options. At the same time, these doctors' past affiliation with the large public hospitals gave Ping An Good Doctor's primary health care immediate credibility, trust, and widespread acceptance by the general public.

To lower the costs of delivering its medical services, Ping An needed scale, which led it to create an internet platform that was easily accessible to people all over the country and would be the sole means of using its primary care services. This allowed it to forgo expensive investments in physical infrastructure such as doctors' offices or outpatient care facilities. With a pool of highly qualified doctors ready to serve people through a low-cost online platform, Ping An offered exceptional buyer value, such as a guaranteed doctor's response in less than thirty seconds, twenty-four-hour accessibility, and two-hour home delivery of all prescriptions, with consultations possible via text and graphics, audio calls, or video calls, and with both the patient and the doctor able to upload and exchange pictures and documents instantaneously. The platform allowed people to access Ping An's services anytime from anywhere at a low cost, offering users never before imagined value.

Ping An Good Doctor's brand-new nondisruptive market of primary care complemented rather than displaced China's hospital-centered health care system. Its high-quality, low-cost, internet-based system supported long-term health management, thereby addressing the chronic and general health needs of a vast population while also alleviating the burden on large public hospitals and allowing doctors there to serve people with serious conditions more productively.

Four years after the company's launch, in August 2018, Ping An Good Doctor went public on the Hong Kong Stock Exchange. It was hailed in the media as a high-tech unicorn with more than 200 million registered users and 32.9 million monthly active users. Today its market cap is greater than $20 billion.

Although Tongwei and Ping An used all three enablers to generate their nondisruptive offerings, the internal resources and capabilities that they already owned and creatively leveraged and newly acquired were essential. In other cases, a nondisruptive offering is created by utilizing external resources and capabilities at zero or very low cost through resourcefulness, with investment focused primarily on building internal resources and capabilities that are distinctive and uniquely appealing to their target buyers.

Square leveraged Apple's iPhone and other smartphones, at no cost to itself, while focusing its internal resources on the Square Reader, the little white plastic hardware device you run your credit card through. Building on Jim McKelvey's design skills (remember, he was an artisanal glassblower), Square created and manufactured the device in-house. The goal was a reader that would not only work but be aesthetically appealing, small, and so cute that it would make people smile and talk about it, so Square's nondisruptive creation would spread via word of mouth. By keeping the design and manufacture in-house, the company could change or refine its hardware's look, feel, and functioning rapidly to correct any problem it encountered as it tested and retested it to get it right.

A "could," not a "should," mindset

Besides resourcefulness and internal resources and capabilities, the third enabler to realize nondisruptive creation is to think and question in terms of "could," not "should." Don't ask what the business model and technology *should be* to realize your nondisruptive creation; ask what they *could be* to turn this into a thriving opportunity. Why? Because "should" is daunting. It's constraining. It freezes our minds and tends to paralyze our creative imaginations by driving us to find *the* answer. And when *the* answer is not immediately evident, as is usually the case, we start to give up. More than that, "should" acts as a sieve that shuts off options instead of allowing us to think freely. Very different ideas that may seem too simple or too "out there" often go unspoken or, worse, don't even enter our mental space, because our subconscious has already written them off when they may in fact be the best idea there is.

"Could," by contrast, energizes us and takes our foot off the pressure pedal. It asks us to think of *possibilities*, not *the* answer, and that gives us permission to think far and wide—as Mohammad Yunus did when looking to unexplored social capital as a way to ensure creditworthiness, or Joan Ganz Cooney did when looking to furry, funny-faced Muppets to replace conventional teachers, or Tongwei did when seeing fish farmers as viable partners for realizing a new green-energy market.

Instead of searching for the ultimate answer, "could" gives you permission to turn over new stones to find possible solutions and pieces to the puzzle—often from unexpected people or places. Recall how Mick Ebeling and his crew turned to a South African carpenter in trying to create 3D arms and hands for young Daniel. "Could" also tempers our instinct to quickly judge every suggestion before it has been duly weighed and considered. Too often we treat our current understanding as though it is permanent when it is often open to change. When we wake up to that fact, we become willing to reconsider our thinking, to be open to the thinking of others, and to question what we may have taken as given and true.

That allows us to step out of the realm of *It can't be done* and into the realm of curiosity, openness, and possibility, where the mechanics of nondisruptive creation are realized.

Let's return to Jim McKelvey and Jack Dorsey. When McKelvey saw an opportunity to leverage the iPhone to process credit card payments, the only accepted method of connecting any piece of electronic hardware to Apple's phone was through its proprietary dock connector, which is what you plug your charger cable into. And to use the dock connector, you had to follow Apple's technical specifications, go through a lengthy approval process, and pay royalties. But "should" didn't interest McKelvey as much as what appeared to be a heretical question at the time: "Could" Square instead use the humble headphone jack to connect the reader to the phone? If Square could make the data of a credit card appear to be the output of the headphone jack, bingo! Square could create a reader that worked with any type of phone—achieving far greater and easier possibilities to scale up and cut costs, since no royalties would need to be paid. That's exactly what Square did. It was the first company in the world to circumvent Apple's dock connector.

A mindset of "could" importantly allows you to bounce back and adjust course when you hit the inevitable roadblocks and hurdles along the way, or the numerous small hitches and problems that are an inescapable part of almost all market-creating innovations, nondisruptive or not. That's because it makes people less attached to their ideas' being right, and more attached to simply realizing the opportunity. So when something doesn't work, the team can far more easily say "next," pivot, and then imagine what they might do instead, expediting the iterative process of trying out specific ideas and ways to realize the opportunity.

Take Prodigy Finance. After it had built a robust, future-oriented risk-return assessment model based on direct historical data about premier MBA schools' postgraduate salaries, jobs, and career performance, Prodigy went to traditional banks to seek funding for its overseas-study loan business. It expected that the model would reassure the banks and give them a new nondisruptive revenue stream. But contrary to their thinking, traditional banks were unreceptive: they were blinded by their existing assumptions and practices, which we elaborated in the previous chapter. Then the 2008 financial crisis set in, and any hope Prodigy had placed in banks completely evaporated. While the financial world came crumbling down, and banks turned their backs on Prodigy, the team didn't throw in the towel despite others' advice to do so.

Rather, the team's creative imagination was fired up by an eager search for where, other than conventional banks, the company could get funding. That's when Prodigy hit on the idea of approaching alumni. Who would know more about the job prospects, starting salaries, and likely career trajectories of fellow graduates of their alma mater than alumni? Alumni would have the money to invest, would understand the funding challenges foreign students faced, and would have confidence in borrowers' ability and motivation to repay their loans. Accordingly, Prodigy approached alumni and succeeded in obtaining their funding to realize its nondisruptive creation.

With solid financial returns and virtually nonexistent default rates, the company then pivoted and leveraged a special-purpose vehicle to issue higher-education student bonds to a far wider network of investors on the Irish Stock Exchange. Soon thereafter banks jumped in, because Prodigy's bonds allowed banks' high-net-worth and family office investors to achieve both solid economic returns and a positive social impact. Prodigy has since expanded to offer loans for MBA, law, engineering, and medical degrees at top schools. As of 2022, the company has loaned more than $1.5 billion to some 30,000 students in more than 850 top-ranking schools in 150 countries.

As with any innovation, in realizing your opportunity, you need to get real market feedback by conducting rapid market tests of your prototype solutions with the very people or organizations your nondisruptive creation aims to help. *Rapid* is the operative word here so that you can create an iterative feedback loop that allows you to learn in real time what works and what doesn't while keeping your financial risk low. A "could" mindset is needed to rapidly experiment and flexibly adjust or pivot your prototype solutions according to the responses of your market tests so that you hit the bull's eye.[3]

Confidence and Competence to Succeed

Collectively, the three building blocks give you a structure for developing the competence and confidence necessary to succeed on the journey of realizing nondisruptive creation. We have frequently seen the mistakes of people whose thinking and ideas on making nondisruptive creation happen were bounded and limited by their internal resources and capabilities. But as we've illustrated, if you are resourceful and have a "could" mindset, you can typically find creative ways to secure the resources, skills, and capabilities you need and are lacking outside your organization. Your competence stems from not only your internal resources and capabilities but also your resourcefulness and mindset.

Besides competence, confidence is equally important. Having a strong collective confidence in the nondisruptive opportunity you've identified and in the specific ideas about how to realize it means that the people involved are intellectually and emotionally

FIGURE 9-2

The confidence-competence map

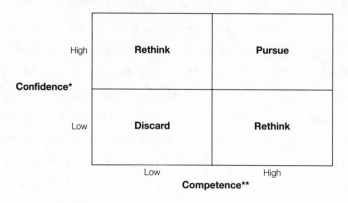

*Collective confidence in an idea
**Resourcefulness, internal capabilities, and a "could" mindset

behind the opportunity and are committed to act on it. When competence meets confidence to act, you put your nondisruptive opportunity on track to succeed. One without the other is not advised, because it lifts your level of risk.

So let us close this chapter with a framework that can help you see the big picture and judge whether you're on the right path. Figure 9-2 shows the confidence-competence map. As seen in the figure, the map has four quadrants, with the x-axis representing competence and the y-axis representing collective confidence. With the map, you need to develop your specific ideas until they arrive at the "pursue" quadrant and have a high chance of success in realizing the opportunity. If those ideas are rated low on both dimensions, and thus fall into the "discard" quadrant, you need to move on to new ones. This is often the case when your team lacks sufficient confidence in the market and/or the impact potential of the nondisruptive opportunity you've identified and the approach

190

and competencies you've brought together to realize it. At this final stage, however, we've often seen that developing specific ideas to realize nondisruptive creation usually starts in one of the two "rethink" quadrants.

Prodigy Finance, for example, had a high level of collective confidence in the market and impact potential of its nondisruptive opportunity and how to realize it. But as we've noted, it hit a competence roadblock with banks in realizing the opportunity. In terms of the map, Prodigy started in the upper-left "rethink" quadrant. As it revised its idea from pursuing banks to getting alumni onboard as a funding source and built a mechanism for global loan enforcement, it moved into the "pursue" quadrant.

In contrast, the Pfizer team behind Viagra had high competence and all the resources and capabilities it needed to realize the nondisruptive opportunity. But the team had to raise the organization's collective confidence to move Viagra from the lower right-hand "rethink" quadrant (high competence, low collective confidence) into the "pursue" quadrant. Recall that the drug generically known as sildenafil, which later became Viagra, was initially developed as a blood-pressure treatment. Its poor performance in blood-pressure trials lent the drug an air of failure, making management and the wider organization jittery and cautious about it. But after building management's collective confidence that the drug could be successfully repurposed for treating ED by conducting an impotency study of the drug and proving its effectiveness, the team behind Viagra succeeded in moving its nondisruptive opportunity into the "pursue" quadrant.

In business as in life, there is no straight line to success. But that doesn't mean success is in any way less inevitable. What it does mean is that you must know where you stand in terms of your confidence and competence, and you must rethink your ideas and actions, as Prodigy Finance and Pfizer did, to take you into the "pursue" quadrant. The confidence-competence map will help you do that.

In our final chapter, we discuss some areas that are ripe for non-disruptive creation and how we can create a compelling future together.

Chapter Ten

Build a Better World
Together

I n your hand, in your phone, with an internet link and a Wi-Fi connection, you have a supercomputer where, with a simple Brave or DuckDuckGo or Google search, you can access knowledge and expertise relevant to virtually any problem you wish to solve or opportunity you aim to create. You can also connect and communicate with millions of people simultaneously or with any single individual—free. Today, the average person with a smartphone and a broadband connection has greater information power than the US government had thirty years ago. This digitally enabled power isn't restricted to an elite few. It is the growing province of an increasing number of people as the digital divide that once separated the rich from the poor, the urban from the rural, and developed nations from less developed ones continues to narrow.

What we ultimately achieve through our imagination and digitally enabled power, however, is dependent on the kind of problems we set out to solve and the kind of opportunities we set out to create. Nondisruptive creation opens a path for all of us to innovate and grow without displacing industries, companies, or jobs—by solving brand-new problems and creating brand-new opportunities beyond existing industry boundaries, whether those problems and opportunities are existing but unexplored or newly emerging.

Consider just a few areas that are ripe for nondisruptive creation in the near future. There's the aging of the world's population—especially the senior bulge in developed nations. As family ties have weakened and the easy mobility of people has led families to live farther and farther apart, seniors are increasingly isolated, living without heartfelt connection and physical touch. This challenging fact of modern life invites nondisruptive opportunities to enrich the physical and emotional lives of the elderly. Likewise, as people live longer, there are new demands for personal care to sustain a healthy and vibrant life: they experience new health challenges that need to be resolved; they need platforms that show them how to leverage the rich wisdom they've accrued through time to create a new, empowering chapter in their lives. And for people of any age who face vital-organ failure, fully functional bioengineered human organs are a nondisruptive opportunity.

As digital technology increasingly penetrates every aspect of our lives, demands for individual sovereignty and new levels of privacy and protection from widespread electronic surveillance are growing rapidly. These issues trigger concerns about the sanctity of our private thoughts and moments and about people's right to express dissenting views. Solutions are needed for new and mounting problems such as the sharing (or blocking) of personal data to influence free elections, politically and ideologically motivated censoring of online news and events, and a breakdown of trust with the costs that accompany it. Efforts to solve these emerging problems will potentially unleash a huge wave of nondisruptive creation.

World energy demand is on track to be 50 percent higher in 2030 than it was in 2016. What's more, with cars increasingly transitioning from fossil fuel to electric, the demand for electricity is expected to explode. Where will this doubling of energy come from, and how will the world meet the growing surge in demand for electricity? Although new energy sources such as wind and sun are increasingly being harnessed, the huge gap between current energy capacity and future needs suggests ample opportunity for the nondisruptive creation of reliable, affordable, and clean new energy sources and for carbon capture in traditional, low-cost energy sources.

Then there is the emergence of rapid urbanization in developing countries, where migration from rural areas to densely populated cities is creating both huge social and economic opportunities and unprecedented problems regarding infrastructure, physical safety, health, community well-being, poverty, and resources. In Africa alone, 800 million people are expected to move into the continent's cities over the next thirty years. These unprecedented, emerging challenges are areas ripe for nondisruptive creation.

We should also think about crucial emerging issues associated with the environment. The rising production of waste, for example, creates ecological issues such as the Great Pacific Garbage Patch, an area three times the size of France that contains more than a trillion pieces of plastic, posing safety and health issues for marine life, damaging our food chain, and destroying the ocean's divine beauty. Such issues present numerous nondisruptive opportunities to create a more sustainable world for ourselves and our children.

As we look beyond Earth and its atmosphere to space, we can imagine a host of nondisruptive opportunities, from mining in space for terrestrial sources of metals in asteroids, to the creation of space travel and even space tourism, to Elon Musk's commitment to create a brand-new opportunity for an interplanetary existence for humans, allowing us to probe deeper into our place in the universe: Are there other species out there? How did we get here? Today Musk and SpaceX are working fervently to realize this nondisruptive opportunity, with the goal of establishing a self-sustaining community on Mars—which in itself would give rise to a wealth of nondisruptive opportunities unimaginable today.

The world is what we make it. The question is not, will these problems be solved or these opportunities created? It is, who will bring us the future and do so in a nondisruptive way that creates growth and prosperity for business and society? We have shared a broad range of nondisruptive-market-creating innovations throughout this book in the hope of highlighting that—as important as disruptive creation has been and will continue to be—the time has come for an expanded view of innovation and growth that expressly recognizes, names, and opens a gateway to what we call nondisruptive creation.

We believe that nondisruptive creation, whether by a little or by a lot, has the potential to serve as a counterbalancing and socially stabilizing economic force as domestic economies and the global economy as a whole thirst for growth but meet the new wave of radically transforming technologies on track to displace a wealth of existing core players, core markets, and current jobs. As we ponder the many challenges faced by our planet and the human race, we will need innovative market-creating solutions. If they can be nondisruptive, not only disruptive, we believe there will be a better chance to bridge the gap between business and society, bringing people together instead of dividing us. We offer not some perfect formula but the start of a fresh conversation and the basic patterns our research revealed to help you identify, unlock, and realize nondisruptive opportunities.

When President John F. Kennedy aimed to build a rocket that could carry a man to the moon and bring him back safely to Earth, he was challenging the United States to reach for nondisruptive creation. This would create a brand-new opportunity that would inspire the nation and demonstrate America's scientific leadership to the world. Many people saw that challenge as little more than a dream, not a realistic opportunity to be created and seized. When asked what it would take to create and seize that nondisruptive opportunity, Wernher von Braun, the leading NASA engineer, answered in five telling words, "The will to do it."[1]

What had appeared impossible, with will and effort became possible. The nondisruptive creation of *Apollo 11* landed humans on the moon on July 20, 1969. Its scale and impact are historic, recognized as "one giant leap for mankind." Like *Apollo 11*, despite the differences in scale and impact, Music: Not Impossible, with which we opened this book, and all the other nondisruptive creations we've discussed challenged our preconceived notions of what could be.

Nondisruptive creation need not be just an intellectual understanding. With the will to make it happen, together with the guidance and frameworks provided here, it can become a more systematic pursuit and reality. We can then take a step toward a better world in which growth for business can be achieved without socially disruptive consequences. It is that hope with which we wrote this book.

Notes

Chapter 1

1. See World Health Organization, "World Report on Vision," 2019.

2. Google Trends show that the relative search interest in the term *disruption* has been on a continuous rise. It has quadrupled over the last score, indicating the increasing popularity for the term. The term was popularized to no small extent by Clayton Christensen's influential work on disruptive technology and innovation. See his seminal work, *The Innovator's Dilemma: When New Technologies Cause Great Firms to Fail* (Boston: Harvard Business School Press, 1997). While his theory is conceived and developed based on low-end disruption as he saw that it causes great firms to fail, the public has been using the term in a broader context to describe the innovation phenomenon where the new displaces the existing market and its incumbents from both low and high ends. It is this common and general understanding of the meaning of disruption that we use here. See endnote 12 for recent research showing that disruption occurs from both the high end and low end of existing markets, as well as originates from both small firms with few resources and established companies with deep pockets.

3. Among many celebrations of disruption, the *Forbes* annual disruption list and CNBC annual Disruptor 50 are good examples.

4. We first formally introduced the theory of nondisruptive creation in an article, W. Chan Kim and Renée Mauborgne, "Nondisruptive Creation: Rethinking Innovation and Growth," *Sloan Management Review,* Spring 2019, 52–60. See also W. Chan Kim and Renée Mauborgne, *Blue Ocean Shift—Beyond Competing: Proven Steps to Inspire Confidence and Seize New Growth* (New York: Hachette, 2017), chapter 2.

5. Nondisruptive creation means that a created offering is nondisruptive to existing industry. It is defined relative to the market not to the firm. When Apple launched its iPod and later iTunes, for example, neither was disruptive to the company; it had no music-playing device or music retail business of its own to displace. However, both were disruptive to existing industry. One disrupted the portable music player industry, while the other did the same to the music retail industry. In our terms, Apple's creation of iPod and iTunes are *not* cases of nondisruptive creation, as they were both disruptive to existing industry.

6. It is important to distinguish between a market solution offered through formal market transactions between sellers and buyers and an informal or nonmarket solution like dirty cloth for menstrual cycles. While sanitary pads eliminated the need for girls to use corn husks or old rags during menstruation, this should not be confused with market disruption, which occurs when an innovative offering displaces an existing industry and the firms in it. Providing a market solution for a problem where only informal or nonmarket solutions exist creates growth without displacing any established market. In fact, many nondisruptive creations occur this way.

7. While scientific invention and technology-driven innovation can generate nondisruptive creation as discussed, they also can generate disruption as in the case of autonomous vehicles versus standard autos or in the case of the scientific inventions of acetaminophen and ibuprofen versus aspirin for most treatments. They should not be confused with and are not interchangeable with nondisruptive creation.

8. The same goes for Viagra, men's cosmeceuticals, 3M Post-it Notes, cell phone accessories, life coaching, and pet Halloween costumes among others.

9. C.K. Prahalad in his influential book *The Fortune at the Bottom of the Pyramid* explained how companies can build and profit from new markets among the world's several billion poorest people, while at the same time helping to alleviate poverty. While his book is not on nondisruptive creation, some new markets exemplified there are nondisruptive as they happen to be created outside existing industry boundaries. Similarly, Christensen, Ojomo, and Dillon showed how market-creating innovation for the previously unserved poor is a path to sustainable prosperity in the case of frontier markets. Evidently, these studies are not about nondisruptive creation. But they are relevant to our research as they suggest the significant potential impact of nondisruptive creation to emerging economies. See, C.K. Prahalad, *The Fortune at the Bottom of the Pyramid: Eradicating Poverty through Profits* (Upper Saddle River, NJ: Wharton School Publishing, 2010). See also, Clayton Christensen, Efosa Ojomo, and Karen Dillon, *The Prosperity Paradox: How Innovation Can Lift Nations Out of Poverty* (New York: Harper Business, 2019).

10. Note that while new-to-the-world products can be nondisruptive, they can also be disruptive, as Uber was to the taxi industry or digital photography was to the film camera industry. Relatedly, Safi Behcall's book *Loonshots: How to Nurture the Crazy Ideas That Win Wars, Cure Diseases, and Transform Industries* (New York: St. Martin's Press, 2019) should not be confused with or seen as discussing nondisruptive creation; loonshots can be both disruptive and nondisruptive.

11. While new goods are not necessarily nondisruptive to existing markets, for discussions on their economic importance, see Timothy Bresnahan and Robert

Notes

Gordon's work, *The Economics of New Goods* (Chicago: University of Chicago Press, 1996). Also see the work of Amar Bhidé, *The Venturesome Economy: How Innovation Sustains Prosperity in a More Connected World* (Princeton, NJ: Princeton University Press, 2008), where he discusses the importance of innovations for creating new goods that are driven by the nondestructive form of entrepreneurship.

12. For example, Glen Schmidt and Cheryl Druehl note, "A disruptive innovation (i.e., one that dramatically disrupts the current market) is not necessarily a disruptive innovation (as Christensen defines the term)." Their research shows two overarching patterns of disruption: low-end encroachment and high-end encroachment with the impact of high-end encroachment on the current market "immediate and striking." See Glen Schmidt and Cheryl Druehl, "When Is a Disruptive Innovation Disruptive?" *Journal of Product Innovation Management* 25, no. 4 (2008): 347–369. Likewise, Sood and Tellis show that disruption arises from not only lower attacks, but also higher attacks, which start out superior to the dominant market offering, demonstrating that disruption of the mainstream market is not limited to low-end or inferior encroachment. See A. Sood and G. Tellis, "Demystifying Disruption: A New Model for Understanding and Predicting Disruptive Technologies," *Marketing Science* 30, no. 2 (2011): 339–354. Joshua Gans also elaborates on how the iPhone disrupted the mobile phone industry from the high end, with the source of disruption not limited to low-end or foothold disruption as Christensen defines it. See Joshua Gans, *The Disruption Dilemma* (Cambridge, MA: MIT Press, 2017). More recently, Muller proposes that for disruption to be a general theory, it needs to embrace high-end disruption as a fact of business reality. See Eitan Muller, "Delimiting Disruption: Why Uber Is Disruptive, but Airbnb Is Not," *International Journal of Research in Marketing* 37, no. 1 (2019). These studies have also shown that disruption need not originate from smaller firms with fewer resources but can also originate from existing companies with deep pockets.

13. See Christensen, *The Innovator's Dilemma*.

14. See Joseph Schumpeter's classic book, *Capitalism, Socialism, and Democracy* (New York: Harper and Brothers, 1942).

15. See Kim and Mauborgne, "Nondisruptive Creation." Relatedly, Joshua Gans, in his review of the literature on disruption, identifies Schumpeter's creative destruction as the conceptual origin of disruption. See Gans, *The Disruption Dilemma*.

16. Disruptive creation, like nondisruptive creation, is defined relative to the market, not to the firm itself.

17. The definition of disruptive creation here is in line with Schumpeter's notion of creative destruction, which "incessantly revolutionizes the economic

structure from *within*, incessantly destroying the old one, incessantly creating a new one." See Schumpeter, *Capitalism, Socialism, and Democracy*, 83.

18. Research on disruption has covered a wide array of issues from why and how disruption occurs, to how to respond to disruptive threats, and to the disruptive mindset. But it has paid scant attention to the negative social externalities that result from disruption. While Schumpeter recognized the social welfare implications of creative destruction, the focus of his study as an economist was more on its long-run impact on economic development and growth. From a business perspective, however, these social costs have significant implications in the way companies balance business and society today and in the future.

19. See Jonah Berger's inspiring book, *Contagious: Why Things Catch On* (New York: Simon & Schuster, 2016).

20. See John Hicks, "The Scope and Status of Welfare Economics," Oxford Economic Papers, new series, 27, November 3, 1975, 307–326.

21. See Paul Romer, "Increasing Returns and Long-Run Growth," *Journal of Political Economy* 94, no. 5 (October 1986): 1002–1037. See also, Paul Romer, "The Origins of Endogenous Growth," *Journal of Economic Perspectives* 8, no. 1 (1994): 3–22.

22. While in the broadest sense, the term *innovation* can be used to describe anything new and/or original, as our prior discussions illuminate, our focus here is limited to innovation that unlocks market creation as it is at the engine of new growth.

23. See W. Chan Kim and Renée Mauborgne, *Blue Ocean Strategy: How to Create Uncontested Market Space and Make the Competition Irrelevant* (Boston: Harvard Business Review Press, 2005; Expanded Edition, 2015).

24. See Kim and Mauborgne, *Blue Ocean Shift*.

25. Schumpeter's focus was on the importance of creative destruction to economic growth, while Christensen's was on the organizational reasons why established companies were caught off guard (or didn't respond) and failed because of them. As Christensen stated in his 2015 interview with Steve Denning, "the concept of disruption is about competitive response; it is not a theory of growth." See Steve Denning, "Fresh Insights from Clayton Christensen on Disruptive Innovation," *Forbes*, December 2, 2015.

26. The concept of *nonconsumption* should not be confused with that of nondisruptive creation. As shown through the disk drive industry example, when the disruptive innovation theory uses the term *nonconsumption* in the context of the untapped low-end fringe market of the industry left out by industry leaders, the theory sees it as an entering foothold for the low-end disrupters that eventually cause industry leaders to fail as they come to dominate the industry. See Christensen, *The Innovator's Dilemma*. In our terms, this is a case of disruptive creation occurring from the low end. On the other hand, when it is used in the context of the frontier

markets where no market solution for their low-end poor exists, the theory sees such nonconsumption situations as opportunities for creating entirely new markets. See Christensen, Ojomo, and Dillon, *The Prosperity Paradox*. In our terms, this is a case of nondisruptive creation in a given area. Depending on the context in which the term *nonconsumption* is used, it can serve as the potential market basis for disruptive creation, blue ocean, or nondisruptive creation. Specifically, when *nonconsumption* exists *within* an existing industry boundary, it serves as the potential market basis for disruptive creation, when it exists *outside* an existing industry boundary, it serves as the basis for nondisruptive creation. Relatedly, its associated idea, jobs to be done, should not be seen as a tool for generating nondisruptive creation. Like *nonconsumption*, depending on the context of where and how the tool is applied, it can help you generate anywhere from disruptive creation to blue ocean strategy to nondisruptive creation. It can even help you significantly improve customer experience so that buyers "fire" the product that they are currently using and "hire" your product. Hence the idea of "jobs to be done," while important, should not be confused with, nor is it equivalent to, nondisruptive creation. See Clayton M. Christensen et al., "Know Your Customers' 'Jobs to Be Done,'" *Harvard Business Review*, September 2016.

Chapter 2

1. Refer to endnote 12 of chapter 1 for recent research establishing that disruption occurs from both the high end and low end of existing markets, as well as from both small firms with few resources and established companies with deep pockets.

2. Buckminster Fuller considered the universe and the dynamic interconnections within it as explaining each and every physical system constituting material existence. Having studied the system of pollination, of how bees in gathering nectar without intention collect pollen and trigger the wider impact of pollination, Fuller set forth what he called the precessional effect where one agent, by taking an action unintentionally, causes consequences to interconnected nodes in the universe. See Buckminster Fuller, *Synergetics* 2 (New York: MacMillan, 1979).

3. Disruption is generally associated with instilling a sense of panic and fear. For example, Joshua Gans, in his excellent book *The Disruption Dilemma* (Cambridge, MA: MIT Press, 2016), muses on how "following the dot com bust 9/11, the world's managers were receptive to a message of fear," consonant with disruption. Likewise, Harvard professor and historian Jill Lepore notes that disruption is "founded on a profound anxiety." Jill Lepore, "The Disruption Machine: What the Gospel of Innovation Gets Wrong," *New Yorker*, June 23, 2014. Among numerous others on the fear of disruption, see Paul Leinwand and Cesare

Notes

Mainardi, "The Fear of Disruption Can Be More Damaging Than Actual Disruption," *Strategy + Business*, September 2017.

Chapter 3

1. See Jim McKelvey's article, "Good Entrepreneurs Don't Set Out to Disrupt," *Harvard Business Review*, May 2020. See also his excellent book, Jim McKelvey, *The Innovation Stack* (New York: Portfolio/Penguin, 2020), which explores the story of Square's creation.

2. Whether disruption occurs from the high end or the low end of an existing market, as discussed in chapter 2, a common success factor is the leap in consumer surplus it delivers over the existing offering.

3. This is formally known as "the replacement effect," a cornerstone of the economic analysis of innovation explored by Kenneth Arrow in his influential article "Economic Welfare and the Allocation of Resources for Inventions," in *The Rate and Direction of Inventive Activity*, ed. R Nelson (Princeton, NJ: Princeton University Press, 1962). The theory holds that there is a reluctance for incumbents to introduce a new product or innovation that would cannibalize and hence replace their existing product or business and the profits that go with it. Incumbents face a disincentive because to gain potential profits of the new, the company must be willing to lose existing profits that are known, discouraging it from disrupting its existing business.

4. Among others, see the excellent research of Michael Tushman and Phil Anderson. Their research found that innovation that is competence-destroying to a firm increases the difficulty for the firm to embrace it. See Michael Tushman and Philip Anderson, "Technological Discontinuities and Organizational Environments," *Administrative Science Quarterly* 31, no. 3 (1986): 439–465.

5. Gans provides an excellent overview and assessment of four ways to manage disruption, noting that each comes with trade-offs and what is more effective is also more costly. Joshua Gans, *The Disruption Dilemma* (Cambridge, MA: MIT Press, 2017).

6. While the "replacement effect" (see endnote 3) provides a disincentive for incumbent firms to respond to disruptive threats or to "disrupt your business before someone else does," this is not the case for nondisruptive creation as it is not reliant on an incumbent destroying its existing business and the profits and growth that go with it.

7. Our point here is that whether a move is disruptive or nondisruptive, standard regulatory scrutiny and actions will exist and likely be greater for certain industry domains. But, in general, nondisruptive creation will likely face less

regulatory and external stakeholder resistance as it is not displacing an existing market and the companies and jobs that go with it.

8. As organizations manage their portfolios to secure profit for today and growth for tomorrow, nondisruptive and disruptive creation are complementary approaches to achieve this. An organization is not relegated to one or the other; the same company, for example, can pursue disruptive creation in one business and nondisruptive creation in another to great effect. SpaceX, for example, has been pursuing not only disruptive creation in reusable rockets and its planned fully reusable Starship but also nondisruptive creation in commercial space travel and building a community on Mars and creating interplanetary existence.

Chapter 4

1. See Milton Friedman's influential article in the *New York Times*, which outlined his central thesis. Milton Friedman, "A Friedman Doctrine—The Social Responsibility of Business Is to Increase Its Profits," *New York Times*, September 13, 1970, https://www.nytimes.com/1970/09/13/archives/a-friedman-doctrine-the-social -responsibility-of-business-is-to.html.

2. Although not without criticism, there has been a steady and pronounced shift from a shareholder- to a stakeholder-centric model of capitalism. In 2019, for example, the US Business Roundtable issued a statement endorsing its commitment to add value to all stakeholders. The statement was signed by over 250 CEOs of America's most powerful corporations, signaling that business is about more than the bottom line. While the tide for stakeholder primacy has been rising across the globe along with pushback at the way it is being imposed, the concern for stakeholders is not new. See, for example, Adolf Berle and Gardiner Means, *The Modern Corporation and Private Property* (New York: Harcourt, Brace, and World Inc., 1932), which espoused that profits were best protected by a long-term view of the good of all. Also, in an early work, Joseph Stiglitz and Sandford Grossman showed that shareholder capitalism did not maximize societal welfare over time, implying a need for more focus on stakeholder concerns. See Sanford Grossman and Joseph Stiglitz, "On the Impossibility of Informationally Efficient Markets," *American Economic Review* 70, no. 3 (1980): 393–408. More recently, among others, Michael Porter and Mark Kramer explore the need for better alignment of business and society (Michael Porter and Mark Kramer, "Creating Shared Value," *Harvard Business Review*, January–February 2011). See also Klaus Schwab and Peter Vanham, *Stakeholder Capitalism: A Global Economy That Works for Progress, People and Planet* (New York: Wiley, 2021), which espouses the need for a shift to stakeholder capitalism.

Notes

3. Oxford Economics, "How Robots Change the World," June 2019, https://www.oxfordeconomics.com/resource/how-robots-change-the-world/.

4. See Mark Muro, Robert Maxim, and Jacob Whiton, "Automation and Artificial Intelligence: How Machines Are Affecting People and Places," Brookings Institution, January 24, 2019.

5. See "The Stockmarket Is Now Run by Computers, Algorithms, and Passive Managers," *Economist*, October 5, 2019.

6. See Carl Benedikt Frey and Michael A. Osborne, "The Future of Employment: How Susceptible Are Jobs to Computerization?" University of Oxford, September 17, 2013.

7. See D. Ardila et al., "End-to-end lung cancer screening with three-dimensional deep learning on low-dose chest computed tomography," *Nature Medicine* 25 (2019): 954–961.

8. See Scott McKinney et al., "International Evaluation of an AI System for Breast Cancer Screening," *Nature* 577 (2022): 89–94.

9. See, for example, OpenAI's DALL-E 2 as well as Midjourney and Stable Diffusion, which all create original images and beautiful art from a description in natural language. All three are able to produce stunning visualizations based on simple and abstract textual descriptions. Beyond answering queries, OpenAI's chatGPT can already compose essays, stories, and even poems. As for music, see for example, OpenAI's Jukebox that generates a wide range of music, or OpenAI's MuseNet that can generate short musical compositions combining styles from country to classical to pop. Irrespective of the creative area, AI's rate of improvement for the most part is steady and rising at an incredible speed.

10. See, among others, Martin Ford, *Rise of the Robots: Technology and the Threat of a Jobless Future* (New York: Basic Books, 2015).

11. See Daniel Susskind's book, *A World Without Work: Technology, Automation, and How We Should Respond* (New York: Metropolitan Books, 2020).

12. As discussed earlier in the chapter, many other pieces will be critical to the puzzle, including upskilling and reskilling, financially supporting the displaced, tax breaks for investments in human capital, and buttressing vulnerable local economies and communities.

Chapter 5

1. While nondisruptive creation is a form of market-creating innovation, the two are not equivalent. As the growth model shows, market-creating innovation is a far broader concept that embraces the full spectrum of new market innovations anchored by disruptive creation on one end of the spectrum and nondisruptive creation on the other.

Notes

2. See W. Chan Kim and Renée Mauborgne, *Blue Ocean Strategy: How to Create Uncontested Market Space and Make the Competition Irrelevant* (Boston: Harvard Business Review Press, 2005, expanded ed., 2015). See also, W. Chan Kim and Renée Mauborgne, *Blue Ocean Shift—Beyond Competing: Proven Steps to Inspire Confidence and Seize New Growth* (New York: Hachette Books, 2017).

3. As technology has driven people to consume media via numerous devices, television viewership across the board has been on the decline for years. However, sports are traditional TV's "saving grace," as sports continue to have among the highest viewership on primetime TV programming. This has not changed nor been disrupted with the advent of e-sports. The most-watched TV show in the United States in the 2019–2020 season was *NFL Sunday Night Football* on NBC, and during the same year, the NBA finals were watched by an average of 7.5 million viewers in the United States (Christina Gough, "Sports on US TV—Statistics & Facts," Statista.com, May 10, 2021). Also, *Sunday Night Football* (NBC) and *Thursday Night Football* (Fox) were the most expensive shows for broadcast TV advertising during the 2020–2021 season in the United States. Data showed that thirty-second spots during these programs were priced at $783,700 and $624,600, respectively (A. Guttmann, "Priciest Shows for Advertisers on Broadcast TV in the U.S. 2020/21," Statista.com, June 2, 2022).

Chapter 6

1. The roots of this idea can be traced to Joe Bain's structure-conduct-performance paradigm. See, among others, Joe S. Bain, ed., *Industrial Organization* (New York: Wiley, 1959).

2. The root of this view can be largely traced to Robert Solow's growth model. For his initial discussion of the model, see the article, "A Contribution to the Theory of Economic Growth," *Quarterly Journal of Economics* 70, no. 1 (February 1956): 65–94, in which Solow demonstrated that technological growth was the key to innovation and long-term economic growth.

3. Joseph Schumpeter, among many others, placed the entrepreneur as the hero and agent of innovation. For his initial introduction of this idea, see Joseph Schumpeter, *Theory of Economic Development* (New York: Routledge, 2021; first published 1911).

4. For the conceptual framing and discussion of this idea, see, among others, W. Chan Kim and Renée Mauborgne, "How Strategy Shapes Structure," *Harvard Business Review*, September 2009, 72–80.

5. The theory of value innovation was introduced and discussed in the context of new market creation. It applies to all forms of market-creating innovation,

nondisruptive creation, blue ocean strategy, and disruption. For the conceptual grounding and in-depth discussion of the theory, among other writings, see W. Chan Kim and Renée Mauborgne, "Strategy, Value Innovation, and the Knowledge Economy," *MIT Sloan Management Review* 40, no. 3 (April 1999): 41–54. For more practical implications, see also W. Chan Kim and Renée Mauborgne, "Value Innovation: The Strategic Logic of High Growth," *Harvard Business Review*, January–February 1997, 102–112.

6. See, among others, Solow, "A Contribution to the Theory of Economic Growth." See also Paul Romer, "Endogenous Technological Change," *Journal of Political Economy* 98, no. 5 (October 1990): S71–S102.

7. See, for example, Sarv Devaraj and Rajiv Kohli, "Performance Impacts of Information Technology: Is Actual Usage the Missing Link?" *Management Science* 49, no. 3 (March 2003): 273–289; and Rajiv Sabherwal and Anand Jeyaraj, "Information Technology Impacts on Firm Performance: An Extension of Kohil and Devaraj (2003)," *MIS Quarterly* 39, no. 4 (December 2015): 809–836.

8. A study conducted based on a 3M experimentation showed that compared with producer innovation generated by its conventional approach, innovation generated by leading-edge users or practitioners was significantly more effective in addressing the problems or opportunities that are new to the world. This 3M experimentation was published in Gary L. Lilien et al., "Performance Assessment of the Lead User Idea Generation Process," *Management Science* 48, no. 8 (August 2002): 1042–1059.

9. See James Surowiecki, *The Wisdom of Crowds: Why the Many Are Smarter Than the Few and How Collective Wisdom Shapes Business, Economies, Societies, and Nations* (New York: Doubleday & Co., 2004). See also, Tom Kelley and David Kelley, *Creative Confidence: Unleashing the Creative Potential Within Us All* (New York: Currency, 2013).

10. On this point, besides Surowiecki, *The Wisdom of Crowds*, see also S. A. Hewlett, M. Marshall, and L. Sherbin, "How Diversity Can Drive Innovation," *Harvard Business Review*, December 2013, 30.

11. Research interview by the authors.

Chapter 7

1. Research interview conducted for the following case study: W. Chan Kim, Renée Mauborgne, and Mi Ji, "Fintech: Innovation without Disruption: How Prodigy Finance Achieved High Growth and Social Good," Case 6523 (Fountaine-bleu, France: INSEAD, 2019), winner of the 2020 EFMD Award for Best Finance and Banking Case.

2. Research interview by the authors.

Chapter 8

1. Research interview conducted for the following case study: W. Chan Kim, Renée Mauborgne, and Mi Ji, "Fintech: Innovation without Disruption: How Prodigy Finance Achieved High Growth and Social Good," Case 6523 (Fountainebleu, France: INSEAD, 2019), winner of the 2020 EFMD Award for Best Finance and Banking Case.

2. See Michael Davis, *Street Gang: The Complete History of Sesame Street* (New York: Penguin Books, 2009), 109.

Chapter 9

1. See Jim McKelvey's excellent book *The Innovation Stack* (New York: Portfolio/Penguin, 2020), where he gives a thorough recount of this and how he and Jack Dorsey effectively applied and leveraged the varied elements of resourcefulness in creating and realizing the Square Reader.

2. McKelvey, *The Innovation Stack*.

3. For a useful resource on rapid prototyping and market testing, see, among others, Eric Ries, *The Lean Startup: How Today's Entrepreneurs Use Continuous Innovation to Create Radically Successful Businesses* (New York: Currency, 2011) and Steve Blank, *The Four Steps to the Epiphany: Successful Strategies for Products That Win* (New York: Wiley, 2020).

Chapter 10

1. See "Science: The Will to Do It," *Time*, June 27, 1977, https://content.time .com/time/subscriber/article/0,33009,915108-1,00.html.

Index

Index

Acknowledgments

As the seventeenth-century English author John Donne wrote, "No man is an island entire of itself; every man is a piece of the continent, a part of the main." No one is self-sufficient; we all rely on others, as has certainly been our case in actualizing this book.

INSEAD, our academic home, has continued to provide a unique and inspiring environment in which to conduct our research. We have benefited greatly from the truly global composition of our faculty, student body, and executive education populations, as well as from the crossover between theory and practice that exists at INSEAD. Dean Ilian Mihov and Deputy Dean Peter Zemsky have provided enduring encouragement and institutional support. Lily Fang, dean of research, has also provided tremendous encouragement and support. Thank you also to Javier Gimeno, dean of faculty, and to Urs Peyer, dean of degree programs, for their support. We would also like to acknowledge our former dean, Frank Brown, for his continuing support of our research.

Warm thanks are especially due to our outstanding team of executive fellows and researchers at the INSEAD Blue Ocean Strategy Institute (IBOSI). While we had help from a highly talented group of researchers over the years, our dedicated executive fellows, Mi Ji, Oh Young Koo, Michael Olenick, and Mélanie Pipino, who have worked with us for the last several years, deserve special mention. Their commitment, drive for perfection, and persistent research support, including case studies, were essential in realizing this book. A researcher beyond those already cited who deserves special mention is Zunaira Munir, who now serves as executive director of the nonprofit Blue Ocean High School Competition, which has become the largest virtual pitch competition in the world for high school students, drawing in students from over 100 countries and growing. Thanks also to our IBOSI coordinator, Rachel Ouhocine.

Special thanks are also due to Jake Cohen, senior associate dean at the MIT Sloan School of Management, for his encouragement and belief in our research, and to all the executives who have willingly given their time in our research journey over the years. Thanks too to all the organizations we've studied that have gone beyond disruption to unleash nondisruptive creation and growth. Thanks also to the many executives and students around the world we've had the privilege to share our research findings with when they were still in the development stage. Their challenging questions and thoughtful feedback clarified and strengthened our ideas.

In our research journey, many people have supported us at different points in our trajectory, and we are thankful for all of them. However, there is one person that stands out in our hearts and minds and deserves special mention: Kasia Duda, the director of Global Media and Relations of the Blue Ocean Global Network. Kasia's unwavering commitment, her dedication to excellence, and her sheer stamina and deep caring have touched us, inspired us, and supported our journey over the last several years. From our hearts to your heart, thank you, Captain. We feel blessed by your presence.

Special thanks are also due to Robert Bong, who leads the Blue Ocean Global Network. Thank you, Dr. Bong, for your guidance and support over the years and for your friendship, which we cherish.

In writing this book we have also benefited from the astute comments of our reviewers at Harvard Business Review Press: Thomas Wedell-Wedellsborg and three other anonymous reviewers. Thank you for your thoughtful comments and feedback, which have strengthened this book.

Finally, we'd like to give special thanks to our long-standing editor at Harvard Business Review Press, Melinda Merino, for her deep belief in our ideas, and to the entire *Harvard Business Review* team. In particular we'd like to thank Editor in Chief Adi Ignatius and the entire Editorial Board Committee for their strong support and encouragement, thoughtful comments, and also for being graciously patient as we struggled to get the manuscript done. Thanks are also due to Martha Spaulding and Jen Waring at HBR Press for their excellent copy editing of the manuscript.

We are grateful to all.

About the Authors

W. Chan Kim and **Renée Mauborgne** are professors of strategy at INSEAD and codirectors of the INSEAD Blue Ocean Strategy Institute in Fontainebleau, France. They are the authors of the global bestseller *Blue Ocean Strategy*, which has sold over four million copies and is recognized as one of the most iconic and impactful strategy books ever written, and *Blue Ocean Shift*, the *New York Times*, #1 *Wall Street Journal*, *USA Today*, and *Los Angeles Times* bestseller. To date, *Blue Ocean Strategy* and *Blue Ocean Shift* teaching materials have been adopted by over 2,800 universities across the globe.

Kim and Mauborgne have published numerous articles in top academic and management journals, including *Academy of Management Journal*, *Management Science*, *Organization Science*, *Strategic Management Journal*, *Administrative Science Quarterly*, *Journal of International Business Studies*, *Harvard Business Review*, and *MIT Sloan Management Review*, as well as articles in the *Wall Street Journal*, the *New York Times*, and the *Financial Times*, among others.

They are the recipients of numerous academic and management awards, including the Nobels Colloquia Prize for Leadership on Business and Economic Thinking, the Carl S. Sloane Award by the Association of Management Consulting Firms, the Leadership Hall of Fame by *Fast Company*, and the Eldridge Haynes Prize for the best original paper by the Academy of International Business, among others. They were named the most influential management thinkers in the world by Thinkers50. To learn more, visit www.blueoceanstrategy.com.